T0195738

Cambridge Elements ≡

Elements in Publishing and Book Culture
edited by
Samantha Rayner
University College London
Leah Tether
University of Bristol

THE SPREAD OF PRINT IN COLONIAL INDIA

Into the Hinterland

Abhijit Gupta

Jadavpur University

CAMBRIDGE
UNIVERSITY PRESS

CAMBRIDGE
UNIVERSITY PRESS

University Printing House, Cambridge CB2 8BS, United Kingdom

One Liberty Plaza, 20th Floor, New York, NY 10006, USA

477 Williamstown Road, Port Melbourne, VIC 3207, Australia

314–321, 3rd Floor, Plot 3, Splendor Forum, Jasola District Centre, New Delhi – 110025, India

103 Penang Road, #05–06/07, Visioncrest Commercial, Singapore 238467

Cambridge University Press is part of the University of Cambridge.

It furthers the University's mission by disseminating knowledge in the pursuit of education, learning, and research at the highest international levels of excellence.

www.cambridge.org
Information on this title: www.cambridge.org/9781108969833
DOI: 10.1017/9781108979870

First published 2021

A catalogue record for this publication is available from the British Library.

ISBN 978-1-108-96983-3 Paperback
ISSN 2514-8524 (online)
ISSN 2514-8516 (print)

The Spread of Print in Colonial India

Into the Hinterland

Elements in Publishing and Book Culture

DOI: 10.1017/9781108979870

First published online: October 2021

Abhijit Gupta

Jadavpur University

Author for correspondence: Abhijit Gupta, abhijit.gupta@jadavpuruniversity.in

ABSTRACT: This study focuses on the spread of print in colonial India towards the middle and end of the nineteenth century. Till the first half of the century, much of the print production in the subcontinent emanated from Presidency cities such as Calcutta, Bombay and Madras, along with centres of missionary production such as Serampore. But with the growing socialization of print and the entry of local entrepreneurs into the field, print began to spread from the metropole to the provinces, from large cities to mofussil towns. This Element will look at this phenomenon in eastern India, and survey how printing spread from Calcutta to centres such as Hooghly-Chinsurah, Murshidabad, Burdwan, Rungpore, etc. The study will particularly consider the rise of periodicals and newspapers in the mofussil, and assess their contribution to a nascent public sphere.

KEYWORDS: printing networks, newspapers, colonial Bengal, Bengali literature, provincial printing

ISBNs: 9781108969833 (PB), 9781108979870 (OC)

ISSNs: 2514-8524 (online), 2514-8516 (print)

Contents

Introduction

This short study is concerned with a somewhat under-reported aspect of book history in India. For understandable reasons, much of the scholarship on book history in the region has had to concentrate on urban centres of print. The first two centuries of the coming of print to India were very much a coastal affair, confined to missionary enclaves such as Goa and Tranquebar (Tharangambadi).[1] Then, with the rise of the East India Company as a political power, the three Presidency cities of Bombay (Mumbai), Madras (Chennai), and Calcutta (Kolkata) became rapidly developing centres of print, as did Serampore, that accidental site of Baptist printing forty kilometres upriver from Calcutta. In the second half of the nineteenth century, the growth of printing in South Asia became phenomenal: 'What had taken Europe three centuries to achieve, the emergence of a full-fledged book culture, was compressed into a single century,'[2] writes Graham Shaw. While the three Presidency cities continued to dominate, a host of other centres of printing began to create their own ecosystems of production and consumption. These included traditional centres of learning, princely states, cantonment towns, local zamindaries, missionary stations, centres of commerce, remote villages and the like.

This study is interested in looking at how print proliferated outside the major, and metropolitan, centres of print in colonial India. This is not a process that can be measured over a limited time-frame, or understood in terms of a set of common parameters. In a country as vast and diverse as India, there is no singular narrative that can be made to accommodate the various networks and flows of print. Neither can a study of a limited length such as this begin to do justice to this narrative. Nevertheless, I have tried to sketch a tentative proposal about how we might enter the space of printing in the hinterland, and understand its dynamics.

---

[1] For historical reasons and ease of quoting, colonial spellings of places have been used in this study, with the modern spelling provided in parentheses when first used. However, when such names are parts of periodicals or presses, the spelling which is closer to the Bengali pronunciation has been used. Example: the city of Dacca, but the periodical *Dhaka prakash*.

[2] Shaw, 'South Asia', 276.

To begin with, I propose a very basic model in understanding the various stages in the proliferation of print, that of networks, flows, and nodes. Thus, centres of print such as Calcutta or Serampore in the early nineteenth century were the starting point of a *network* that would eventually enable print to disperse into the hinterland. This network may be defined as the sum of the processes and personnel connected with the production of print, as well as those agents who were responsible for the distribution of the printed product. Further, the printing emanating from such centres would necessarily be heterogeneous and multilingual in scope. The second element in this model would be designated *flows*, consisting of not just the circulation of the printed products, but also of personnel – printers, type-makers, binders, booksellers, authors, journalists, correspondents – whose mobilities were key to the formation of the third component of this model: *nodes*. It is in the formation of such nodes of printing that we might locate the meaningful dispersion of the print into the hinterland. As we will see, many of these nodes would develop into networks in their own right, while others would restrict themselves to a limited sphere of operations before ultimately petering out.

Using this model, this study tries to identify key moments and episodes in the creation of local economies of print. In the first instance, we consider the flow of the printed book from centres of print into the hinterland. This stage was largely a missionary enterprise, with tracts or books of the Bible being circulated free of cost over much of India, through the elaborate missionary network of first preachers, and later, colporteurs. Then, towards the end of the second decade of the nineteenth century, the missionaries were joined by the local intelligentsia and a section of the colonial administration in creating textbooks and pedagogical literature for primary and secondary classrooms. These too circulated by way of the missionary networks as well as new networks created by the colonial apparatus. Though information about such flows is scarce and erratic – and almost entirely dependent on the missionary and imperial archives – they nevertheless enable us to put together a very preliminary map of reading and readers' responses, and trace the early history of the socialisation of print in the Indian subcontinent.

In the second stage of this study, we will look at specific nodes of printing that came into being in the hinterland from roughly the 1840s onwards. This was very much a stop-start process, with the usual quota of false dawns and aborted beginnings. Key to this process was the availability of both printing machinery and the expertise necessary to run it, away from the usual centres of printing. This is a crucial moment in the hitherto unidirectional flow of workers, skills and material into the city. With the rise of Calcutta as a hub of commerce and imperial power, a steady stream of primarily upper-caste Hindus flowed from the countryside into the city, looking for white-collar jobs under the Company. They formed the lower cadre of the law courts, merchant offices, chambers of commerce and educational institutions, and also found employment in the nascent publishing industry. But is it possible to identify a moment when the flow ceased to be unidirectional, and the skills acquired in the city began to find their way back into the hinterland? In his work on peripatetic printers during the Victorian age, David Finkelstein poses a number of questions that may fruitfully be posed in the context of colonial India as well: 'What infrastructures and mechanisms underpinned such print culture developments? What cultural values and trade skills were transmitted and embedded in indigenous settings by workers who flowed through established and developing territories? ... How did locals and incomers alike deal with each other in such work spaces?'[3] These questions become crucial when we try to understand how local economies of print came into being and were sustained.

The Case of Colonial Bengal

In order to study the above phenomena, I have chosen undivided Bengal of the nineteenth century as an exemplar. Among other things, Bengal lends itself particularly well to the model proposed above owing to the presence of not one, but two, major networks of print during this period. The first is Serampore, formerly a Danish enclave, and for that reason the site of a Baptist mission (the East India Company was famously allergic to missionaries operating in their bailiwick), which from 1800 expanded into one

---

[3] Finkelstein, *Movable Types*, 5.

of the most prolific centres of print production in all of South and Southeast Asia. The elaborate missionary network that ramified from Serampore, towards the west, as well as the south-east, carried with it a stream of tracts and Bibles, which were handed out to all comers wherever their proselytisers went. Unfortunately, there is not a great deal of information in the otherwise copious missionary archives about those who might have actually read the tracts and Bibles, other than a handful of overly dramatic accounts of Indians taking to Christianity. But distribution of print on such a large scale (by one estimate, six million tracts were distributed during 1823–68) is bound to leave traces, and the first part of the study tries to compile a tally of such traces and evidence. We are in somewhat better documented territory when we look at the dispersion of textbooks by societies such as the Calcutta School-Book Society (CSBS), which started operations in 1817. As I have argued elsewhere,[4] the CSBS's activities presaged Macaulay's Englishing of the imperial curriculum by nearly two decades. More importantly for this study, it established a robust network of distribution facilitated by inspector of schools, their agents, and sub-agents. In the first chapter, therefore, I look at the twin networks of print put into place by the Serampore Baptists and the CSBS respectively.

In the second chapter, we look at the dispersal of print production from the city to its hinterland, taking Calcutta as the point of departure. Along with Bengali, the lingua franca of the lower delta of Bengal, the Calcutta press printed extensively in languages such as Persian, Hindustani (Urdu), Hindi, Nepali, Odia, Assamese, Tibetan, Burmese and English, to name a few. These have been well documented by scholars. But this chapter will focus on what we might call small town or 'mofussil' presses as they originated outside Calcutta, from roughly the mid-century onwards. Such a survey will enable us to identify a wide range of printing models and practices that called for a degree of innovation and reinvention. While the famed Battala quarter of Calcutta was the locus of the commercial book market, the districts provided a congenial environment for alternative modes of print production and consumption. In particular, the periodical press flourished in the districts, providing a bracing counterpart to the

---

[4] Gupta, 'The Calcutta School-Book Society'.

public discourse emanating from the city. In contrast, book publishing with the attendant cachet of authorship was more of a metropolitan phenomenon, and continues to be so till this day. Of course, the mortality and morbidity rate of districts presses and publications were high, but that should not detract from their efforts to forge micro-communities of textual production, and to address local issues and concerns.

I should mention here that I use the word 'mofussil' as both a descriptive and conceptual category. In the first sense of the mofussil, one can do no better than to turn to that old chestnut *Hobson-Jobson*: "'The provinces," – the country stations and districts, as contra-distinguished from 'the Presidency'; or, relatively, the rural localities of a district as contra-distinguished from the sudder or chief station, which is the residence of the district authorities. Thus if, in Calcutta, one talks of the Mofussil, he means anywhere in Bengal out of Calcutta.'[5] But, in the Bengali language, the word also carries an affective charge that obtains to this day. Along with a sense of location, the word mofussil variously functions as a site of memory, a mood and a positional politics, especially with reference to the cultural counterweight that is Calcutta.

What were the chief centres of such printing in undivided Bengal, or the Bengal Presidency?[6] Closest to Calcutta were riverside towns such as Hooghly, Chinsurah (Chuchura), Serampore, and Naihati in the Hooghly district, followed by Burdwan (Bardhaman), in the district of the same name. Two hundred kilometres north of Calcutta lay the twin towns of Murshidabad and Berhampore. As we move into the eastern part of Bengal, the most pre-eminent centre of printing was Dacca (Dhaka), with Mymensing, Rungpore (Rangpur), Sylhet (Srihatta) and Jessore following suit. Additionally, we see the rise of printing in those parts of undivided Bengal where Bengali was not the dominant language: Odia printing in Cuttack and Balasore, Assamese printing in Sibsagar and Goalpara, and Hindi and Urdu printing in Patna and Arrah. Finally, there were centres of

---

[5] Burnell and Yule, *Hobson-Jobson*, 435.

[6] The Bengal Presidency, an administrative unit of colonial India, consisted of parts or whole of the following modern-day states/nations: Assam, Bangladesh, Bihar, Meghalaya, Odisha, Tripura and West Bengal.

Bengali diaspora such as Benaras (Varanasi) and Allahabad outside Bengal, and Bhagalpur and Hazaribagh situated towards the western perimeter of the undivided Bengal.

What were the languages in which printing took place? While the towns in the vicinity of Calcutta printed mostly in Bengali, the linguistic map became more diverse as the distance increased from Calcutta. Also, typography was not the only technology for printing. Ulrike Stark points out how lithography, after originating in Calcutta in the 1820s, spread 'right across Upper India' as the technology of choice, particularly for printing in Urdu and Persian.[7] According to Francesca Orsini, lithography enabled presses to print in a number of languages, 'for the book needed only to be copied in a fair hand in the other script'.[8] Thus, presses in Patna and Arrah (now in the state of Bihar) were able to print in four languages – Arabic, Hindi, Persian and Urdu – employing both lithography and typography. As far as district presses in middle and lower Bengal were concerned, they were overwhelmingly typographic, and usually printed in one, or at most two, languages. This was owing to the limited resources a small press would possess, as well as the limited readership they would cater to.

Printing in other regional languages was the preserve of missionaries before indigenous entrepreneurs entered the fray. Before the setting up of the Orissa Mission Press in 1838 in Cuttack, printing in Odia was carried out by the two Baptist presses in Serampore and Calcutta. The coming of missionaries such as Bampton, Pegg, Sutton and Lacey to Odisha resulted in widespread distribution of tracts, following the Serampore model. Till 1866, the Cuttack Mission Press was the only centre of printing in Odisha, printing hundreds of tracts and other titles in a variety of subjects. Like the Serampore press, it trained up a whole generation of print-house personnel – by 1858, it employed as many as eighteen people in the press.[9] But within two years of each other, two indigenous establishments were set up – the Cuttack Printing Co. of Gourishankar Ray in 1866, and the Utkal Press of Fakir Mohan Senapati in Balasore (Baleshwar) in 1868 – which carried the

---

[7] Stark, *An Empire of Books*, 46.   [8] Orsini, *Print and Pleasure*, 17

[9] Shaw, 'The Cuttack Mission Press', 41.

bulk of Odia printing in the nineteenth century. Assamese too had a trajectory similar to Odia, with missionaries setting up a press in Sadiya in 1836. This later shifted to Sibsagar, from where the missionaries printed the influential periodical *Orunodoi* from 1846. Owing to Assamese using the same typeface as Bengali, much of early printing in the language was carried out from Calcutta presses, before take-up by presses in Assam from the 1870s. Presses such as the Chidananda Press at Guwahati, the Hitasadhani Press at Goalpara and the Dharmaprakash Press at Jorhat became active both in book and periodicals printing,

Reading the Archives

The material in the first chapter is almost entirely drawn from institutional histories and archives – in particular, those of the Mission Press of Serampore, and the CSBS. The second chapter is able to bring a wider variety of sources into play, such as the publications of the Bengali press, memoirs and biographies, government reports, bibliographies, catalogues and the like. However, the single largest body of information about book printing of the period are the multi-volume Bengal Library Catalogues, issued four times a year following the passage of the Press Registration Act, or Act XXV of 1867, which made it compulsory for printers to register all their publications with the government, book, periodical or newspaper.

Given that much of the book – particularly the first chapter – is dependent on missionary and imperial archives of the first quarter of the nineteenth century, certain caveats are necessary, especially in relation to missionary archives. Given the near-total absence of any indigenous records and testimonies for this period, we have to be cautious about how we interpret missionary publications and records. For example, despite copious records left by the missionaries about almost all aspects of their work, there is a complete lack of mention of large chunks of their print output. Understandably, Bibles and tracts publications are reported upon in detail, as these were largely paid for by donations, and there was a need to account for how such monies were spent. But the missionaries also carried out other kinds of printing, such as those for Fort William College, or the

CSBS. These find nearly no mention in their despatches. Early in the 1800s, the Mission Press produced the first-ever printed versions of the Sanskrit epics the *Ramayana* and the *Mahabharata*, in the Bengali translations of Krittibas Ojha and Kasiram Das respectively. The archives are completely silent about this significant initiative. The same is true of the incomplete 1806 prose translation in English of the *Ramayana* carried out by Carey and Marshman, a project financed by the Asiatic Society of Calcutta.

Then there is the question of erasures. Despite working with a large supporting staff of local scholars, translators and print-house personnel, the missionaries rarely thought it fit to mention them by name. Wages for unnamed 'pundits in different languages' were a regular feature of the balance-sheet printed by the missionaries. The only occasion on which staff members were named was when they had converted to Christianity – thus, in 18ll, we have the name of eight print-house staff, all converts. Gangakishore Bhattacharya, the first Bengali to set up as publisher learnt his trade at the Mission Press but is never named in the despatches. Likewise, one looks in vain for meaningful references to the two great typemakers who worked at Serampore, Panchanan and Manohar Karmakar. These erasures are frustrating as the names of these workers trained at Serampore could have given us a much clearer idea about the beginnings of the indigenous book trade.

In comparison, the bureaucratic and impersonal imperial archive is more comprehensive. However, Samarpita Mitra alerts us that a database such as the *Bengal Library Catalogue* is also marked by its own share of omissions as publishers often submitted incomplete returns, though such omissions are likely to have been very few. She also draws our attention to the 'Western classificatory' schemes that were used to classify Indian literary output, thereby reflecting a colonial epistemological imperative.[10] A. R. Venkatachalapathy is more forthright in referring to the 'bureaucratic stupidity' of the classification and the overall diminishing returns of the quarterly reports from the 1920s.[11]

~

[10] Mitra, *Modern Literary Culture*, 32.

[11] Venkatachalapathy, *Province of the Book*, 175–6.

Prologue: The Three Journeys of Gangakishore Bhattacharya

On a morning sometime in the early years of the nineteenth century, a man named Gangakishore Bhattacharya might have been found journeying to the Danish enclave of Serampore, from his native village Bahara. It would have been a considerable journey by either foot or bullock-cart, more so by the river – today, it would take nearly three hours to drive the 100 km distance via National Highway 19.

Why was Gangakishore travelling to Serampore? He might have heard that three *sahebs* (lit. white men) had set up a Baptist mission on the banks of the Hooghly river. Or he might have heard one of the brethren preach as they went up the river. In any case, there was work for such a one as Gangakishore. Under the leadership of the 'Serampore Trio' – William Carey, Joshua Marshman and William Ward – the mission had set up its own printing press in 1800 and was intent on publishing the Bible in as many languages as possible. The press needed workers, and many came from near and far to work in the print shop, the bindery and the type-foundry.

We do not know how long Gangakishore apprenticed at Serampore. William Ward, who was himself a printer, remarked: '(F)or about a month at first we had a brahman compositor, but we were quite weary of him.'[12] This is unlikely to refer to Gangakishore, and later accounts convey a different impression. George Smith, biographer of William Carey, wrote: 'The first Bengali, who on his own account, printed works in the vernacular on trade principles, was Gunga Kishore, whom Carey and Ward had trained at Serampore.'[13]

At an unknown date, Gangakishore made his second and much shorter journey, this time to Calcutta. At that time, there were no Indian-owned printing presses in the city, other than the Sanksrit Press of Baburam Sharma, a faculty member at Fort William College,[14] and a handful of the so-called 'maulvi presses', which also printed for the Fort William College list. In Calcutta, Gangakishore found employment with Ferris & Co.,

---

[12] Smith, *William Carey*, 253. [13] Ibid., 274.

[14] The Fort William College was set up in 1800 to train the future cadre of the Company.

a printing press set up by Paul Ferris. In 1802, Ferris & Co. were also acting as Calcutta agents for the Mission Press at Serampore,[15] and Gangakishore may have made contact with them while training at Serampore.

We find Gangakishore branching out on his own in 1816, publishing three titles in one year from the Ferris Press under his own name. These were *Ingreji byakaran* (English grammar), *Daybhaag* (Hindu inheritance law), and the famed *Annadamangal* and *Bidyasundar*, a courtly romance by Bharatchandra Ray and the first Bengali book to be accompanied by wood-cut illustrations.[16] In the next few years, he added more titles to his list,[17] and famously co-founded the first-ever Bengali periodical with Harachandra Roy, the *Bangal gejeti*, in 1818.[18] These facts are well known and do not require reiteration.

However, what is less known is the fact that the Ferris Press had issued a bilingual title in 1815, in which Gangakishore had played a somewhat different role from usual. This was new edition of John Miller's 1797 *The Tutor: in English and Bengalee*,[19] a work aimed at teaching English to Bengali learners. Ferris reissued the work in 1815, but with the addendum: *Carefully revised and corrected by a professional pundit. Re-printed from a work formerly published by the late Mr. John Miller.* Now who might be he professional pundit? There is no mention of any name on the title-page, but if one looks at two-page Bengali preface to the work, the name of Gangakishore emerges as the pundit in question.

The preface, written by Gangakishore himself, is remarkable in several aspects. It is written in the traditional songlike Bengali *payar* cadence of loosely rhyming couplets. After the ritual invocation of Brahma, Gangakishore announces his intention to amend the previous work,

[15] Shaw, *Printing in Calcutta*, 48.

[16] For a detailed study of the many lives of Bharatchandra's opus, see Roy, *Journey of Bidyasundar*.

[17] For a description of his printing career in Calcutta, see Brajendranath, 'Gangakishore Bhattacharya', *SSK* 1, 158–170.

[18] Unfortunately, there are no extant copies of this periodical.

[19] I am grateful to Richard Kossow for allowing me to quote from this rare – and to my knowledge – unique title.

which had apparently been written in a hurry and where it is hard to separate the Bengali from the English. This is followed by Gangakishore identifying himself by name, and claiming lawful habitation in Bardhaman. The address is then further narrowed to a riverside habitation in the 'charming village Bahara', on whose opposite bank stood the village of Agradwip. The protocol that Gangakishore deploys here is that of the scribal colophon, where it was customary for the scribe to provide information about his location and antecedents. But it also appears that the preface is an eloquent plea for authorial recognition, where Gangakishore is seeking to bypass the anonymity of the 'professional pundit' on the title-page.

After falling out with his partner Harachandra Ghosh in 1818–19, Gangakishore made his final journey back to his native village Bahara, but this time with a printing press in tow. It is very likely that this is the first-ever instance in nineteenth-century Bengal – or indeed, India – of setting up a printing press away from the metropolis. By this time, Gangakishore had become quite famous and the *Friend of India* newspaper wrote admiringly in 1820: '(H)e printed several works at the press of a European, for which having obtained a ready sale, he established an office of his own, and opened a book shop. . . . (H)e has now removed his press to his native village. He appointed agents in the chief towns and villages to Bengal, from whom his books were purchased with great avidity.'[20] In Bahara, he seems to have printed at least five titles from the Bangal Gejeti press: a reprint of a book of Bengali regulations in 1820;[21] a volume on medicine titled *Cikistarnab* in the same year; the *Drabyagun* in 1824; and in the same year, the second edition of the *Bhagabadgita*, first published in 1820. The printing of *Bhagabadgita*, a seminal Hindu text, in the Sanskrit original accompanied by a Bengali prose translation, is an important moment in the early history of print in the region. This is one of the first attempts to produce a sacred Hindu text by the alien and potentially contaminating technology of printing, a process

---

[20] 'The Native Press', 123.

[21] *The Bengalee Regulations for Maul, Dewany and Phaujdary Adalut for the year 1818*, by P. M. Lynch, printed in 'Buhuraw' in 1820, 're-printed by Gungakissore Bhauttacharge'.

which would be carried on by Bhabanicharan Bandyopadhyay.[22] It is surmised that Gangakishore died before 1831, though his press in Bahara reportedly continued to print till at least 1844.[23]

A look at Gangakishore's eclectic list seems to suggest that it was targeted at a readership that was highly literate, catering to both older and more recent textual regimes. The titles on medicine, inheritance, courtly romance and the scriptures seem to address a readership well-versed in the protocols of the manuscript book, while those on language learning and regulations were responses to emerging forms of knowledge. As Anindita Ghosh has suggested, a text such as *Annadamangal* was already familiar to a preprint readership, and most early Bengali presses chose their titles with this readership in mind.[24] Gangakishore's alertness to both sectors of the incipient print market would in time become a commonplace of the book trade of the city, which faced no difficulty in servicing different sectors of the market. But it would take much longer to emulate Gangakishore's other feat of building a bridge between the city and the village. He worked first with missionaries and Europeans, then branched out on his own; printed books as well as arguably the first-ever periodical in Bengali; was commercially successful both in the city and away from it. Crucially, he did so at a time when the printed book had not been wholly socialised and a novelty to most who encountered it. He could not have known it at that time, but Gangakishore had already laid down the trail which print in Bengal would follow.

---

[22] For a more detailed discussion on this, see Chakravorty, 'Purity and Print'.

[23] Brajendranath, 'Gangakishore', *SSC* 1, 170.

[24] Anindita Ghosh, 'Coming of the Book', 36.

1 Out of Serampore

We begin with a simple question: how did the voluminous output of the Mission Press at Serampore make its way to readers? Those familiar with the history of printing in that erstwhile Danish enclave will be aware that at least two-thirds of all Bibles produced in South and Southeast Asia in the first three decades of the nineteenth century emanated from its Mission Press. Not counting tracts, the number of Bibles amounted to 212,565 volumes over thirty-two years, according to a calculation by the missionaries themselves in the so-called Tenth Memoir of 1834.[25] Three decades later, the Rev. John Murdoch would carry out a census of 'Christian vernacular literature' in India. In Bengal alone five missionary bodies were engaged in publishing tracts and Bibles. These were the Serampore missionaries, the Calcutta Baptist Mission Press, the London Missionary Society, the Church Missionary Society and the Calcutta Christian Tract and Book Society (CCTBS). Murdoch added approximately 210,000 tracts to the total tallied by the Serampore brethren. The Baptists of Calcutta accounted for over 50,000 tracts between 1818 and 1842. The London Missionary Society chipped in with nearly 100,000. But the most prolific printer of tracts was the CCTBS, which accounted for a mammoth 5,190,340 tracts between 1823 and 1868. And these are not all the figures – there were other bodies like the Bishop's College Press and the Church Mission that accounted for more copies. And this was just the Bengal Presidency. Elsewhere, there were bodies like the Benaras Tracts Society, Agra and North Indian Tract Societies, Bombay Tract Society, the American Mission Press Allahabad, the Punjab Tract Society, the Ludhiana Mission, the Secundra Orphan Press, the Tiroot Mission, the Amritsar Mission, the Bombay Tract Society, the Madras Tract Society and so on.

On the basis of such evidence, India should have been awash with tracts. And to a certain extent, it was. The missionaries believed in handing out tracts – and on occasion, whole Bibles – to pretty much anyone who asked for them. But it is notoriously difficult to track where they went to. The

---

[25] *Tenth Memoir*, 61.

missionaries on occasions tried half-heartedly to keep a tally of which tracts went where. The Serampore missionaries, for instance, published a regular return under the column 'Gratuitous Distribution' in their memoirs. But such attempts could also cause unease among mission circles, if someone did the arithmetic of the very poor rate of conversions achieved in relation to the expenditure on the translation and printing of tracts. The Serampore model of fundraising rested squarely on persuading donors to contribute for the printing of the Bible in 'native tongues' – sooner or later there would be questions about what the funds had achieved.

From the point of view of this study, the distribution of tracts can tell a different story – that of the spread and gradual socialisation of print in the hinterland. At the same time, we have to be careful about jumping to conclusions about the beginning of a reading community. For there is little evidence that the tracts that were so eagerly received were actually read, or even recognised as textual objects. In certain cases, the book might have been recognised as a religious object, or occasionally, fetishised as such. In a celebrated and much-translated book called *Voyages and Travels of a Bible*, written by John Campbell in 1818, the career of a copy of the New Testament is traced, from a bookshop to a county gentleman's library in England, then from Liverpool to the West Indies, then falling into the possession of a slave who sells it to a bookshop, then read to slaves and so forth, finally washing up via the Gulf of Mexico in a North American port, all battered and illegible. But throughout its journeys, the book is valued for its textual or semantic charge. In India, this did not necessarily happen – here, the Christian book was first fetishised as object, and only then, if at all, as text. Occupying an ambiguous position between commodity and gift, the missionary book entered into a wholly material relationship with its intended consumers, but in a way that often served to confute the missionary agenda in which the book must necessarily be configured as text. In India, the practice of distributing tracts indiscriminately yielded poor returns in terms of conversions, and it was often bemoaned at missionary conferences that most Indians who took the printed word so eagerly from them would use the paper as wrappers or waste, a practice of recycling and repurposing that exists to this day.

True to Type

The setting up of the mission and the printing of the New Testament in Bengali in 1800 from Serampore is too well-known to merit repetition. But what is significant is the association of the missionaries – especially William Carey – with the newly set-up Fort William College in Calcutta, also established in 1800. While the relationship between the Company and the missionaries was fraught till at least 1813 (the Charter Act of 1813 renewed the East India Company's rule in India, and relaxed restrictions on missionary activities in India, among other things), there was an occasional convergence of interests, such as when Carey was asked to head the departments of Sanskrit and Bengali at the college. He also had to write the textbooks for classroom teaching, and publish them from the Mission Press. Thus, from the very beginning, there were two distinct streams of printing from the press, of tracts and textbooks. Though targeted at very different readerships, both played significant roles in sending the printed book afield.

But even within the broad category of tracts and Bibles, there were significant differences. In the early years of the Mission Press, we can distinguish three categories of publications, with different target audiences. The first, and the most prestigious, were the biblical translations, either of the entire Old and New Testaments, or the books thereof. Though these were sometimes given out by preachers in the field, they were more in the manner of legacy documents, either to be placed in libraries and collections, or sent to parent and funding bodies. Then there were the tracts, meant to be distributed free to all comers. These would consist of catechisms, dialogues, call to prayers, sermons, Christian biographies and the like. But a very considerable number of such tracts – rarely longer than two or three formes – were devoted to hymns and songs. A preacher who could carry a tune – such as John Chamberlain or the 'native catechist' Anund Messeh – was clearly an asset, and it can be surmised that the 'first contact' with print for many would have been through song. In such an overwhelmingly oral milieu, the printed text would be more symbolic than functional, intended to proclaim a 'superior' technological order and evoke a sense of awe.

The textbooks, written for and funded by the Fort William College, served an entirely different reader, the would-be colonial administrator, and it is in this sector that the congruence between the imperial and the missionary agenda is more clear. For example, in October 1803, Odisha was annexed to British dominion, and the missionaries – in anticipation of a new mission field – began translating the Bible into Odia, with the aid of an Odia pundit. Carey also began a Maratha grammar as Lord Wellesley decided to introduce that language into the college's curriculum for those who would serve in the Bombay Presidency. In order to print in all these languages, new type had to be cast, which could then be used for printing both college textbooks as well as Christian literature. The Serampore Mission was particularly fortunate in this respect – Panchanan Karmakar, the smith who had cut the Bengali font for the Bengali New Testament, had passed on in 1803, but his apprentice Manohar Karmakar was even more skilful and 'continued to make elegant founts of type in all eastern languages for the mission and for sale to others for more than forty years'.[26] After Bengali, the next font to be cast was the Devanagri and its first fruit was a Marathi grammar, issued in 1805, intended for students of Fort William College. By 1807, translations in eleven languages were in hand, with six translations – in Bengali, Odia, Sanskrit, Marathi, Hindustani and Persian – in press.

Strangely enough, the version on which the missionaries had pinned their highest hopes was the Sanskrit New Testament. On 6 June 1806, William Ward had noted:

> We have begun to print the Shanscrit Testament, the publication of which is of great importance, as a faithful translation into this language will render translations into other Eastern languages easy and certain. Every Eastern pundit knows the Shanscrit, and could make from it a good translation into his own vernacular tongue. By translating the scriptures therefore into this language we, in effect, translate them into all languages of Asia.[27]

[26] Smith, *William Carey*, 182.   [27] Stennett, *William Ward*, 151.

This was a vaunting ambition, but the missionaries laboured under the impression that most Indian languages were derived from a common stock and that, 'in them all, the construction, the phraseology, the idiom, the imagiary [sic] are nearly similar'.[28] The memoir of 1808 mooted the hiring of pundits in other languages who would use Bengali as the source language, superintended by a European. This stratagem was trialled with the Odia New Testament, which though bearing 1807 on the title-page, was actually completed in 1809, in the same year in which the Sanskrit New Testament was issued. In their first-ever 'Memoir' or conspectus of work done, the missionaries remarked: 'In the Orissa we have been compelled also to cast a new font of types, as none before existed in that character. The font consists of about 300 separate combinations, and the whole expense of cutting and casting has amounted to at least 1000 rupees'.[29] The other font Serampore was able to cast successfully was the Modi font for printing in Marathi. As A. K. Priolkar points out, there were two Maratha scripts – the Balbodh, or the Nagari, which was used for more classical and literary works, and the Modi, used for correspondence, business, etc. Without naming the font as Modi, the missionaries reported on much the same thing:

> Although in the Mahratta country the Devanagari character is well known to men of education, yet a character is current among the men of business which is much smaller, and varies considerably in form from the Nagari, though the number and power of the letters nearly correspond. We have cast a font in this character, in which we have begun to print the Mahratta New Testament, as well as a Mahratta dictionary.[30]

Armed thus with a repertoire of typefaces, the Mission Press was now in a position to set their sights beyond Bengal.

---

[28] *Translation of the Scriptures*, 16. [29] *Translations of the Sacred Scriptures*, 19.
[30] Ibid., 19–20.

Spreading the Net

We now turn to the question of the distribution of missionary literature, and in particular the vexed question of 'gratuitous distribution' of tracts. As Carey shouldered the twin responsibilities of the Fort William College and the Mission Press, and Marshman and Ward looking after translations and printing respectively, the task of preaching and distributing tracts fell on the younger brethren. One of the most active – though ill-starred – among them was John Chamberlain, who had arrived from Northampton in June 1803. Chamberlain had a gift for languages and an ear for music, both invaluable attributes in a preacher. But he was not always amenable to mission discipline, and Carey soon felt that he would be better engaged away from Serampore. On 27 February 1804, he wrote to Fuller: 'We have agreed to make an experiment . . . to extend the mission, by setting up several subordinate stations, at about one hundred miles from each other . . . Brother Chamberlain will be fixed in the first, which we intend to form immediately near Cutwa, on the banks of the Calcutta river, above Nuddea'.[31]

Chamberlain's accounts of his wanderings in Bengal, and later into the Hindi heartland, provide us with one of the earliest accounts of the Christian book making its way into the hands of its readers. Here are some early entries from his journals, typical of the mission model of preachers into the field:

> - 10 Jan. 1804. Olooberia: They were very eager for our papers; some asked for books, i.e. Testaments: we left two there, and a copy of the Psalms.
> - 11 Jan. 1804. Kulpee: Here we left many tracts and hymns, seven testaments, three or four copies of the Books of Psalms; and the people were very desirous to have more.
> - 7 Feb. 1804. I, my dear wife, and Krishno left Serampore for Dinagepore, whence Krishno proposes to proceed to Benares . . . he has taken with him a number of Hindoostanee tracts.[32]

[31] Carey, *William Carey*, 356. [32] Yates, *John Chamberlain*, 124–32.

Between January and March 1804, Chamberlain made two journeys, the first to Gangasagar, a river island near the Bay of Bengal and the site of gathering of Hindu pilgrims every January, and second towards Dinajpur and Murshidabad in northern Bengal. The distribution of papers (tracts) and books (Bibles) would be carried out in public places such as bazaars, fairs, festive occasions, river *ghats* and the like. Such distribution would usually be preceded by preaching, which would invariably draw large crowds, in the main attentive and occasionally disruptive. From the detailed accounts Chamberlain provides of his disputations with his audience, it is clear that at this point print is very much an outlier on a battleground that is overwhelmingly oral, comprising speech, argument and sometimes song.

But trouble began to brew once the missionaries began to expand their sphere of activities. The Vellore Mutiny of 10 July 1806 – in which attacks on and killings of British troops in Vellore Fort were followed by summary executions of the mutineers – were attributed by certain quarters to Indian resentment at missionary activities. Carey was summoned before the Supreme Court on 26 August 1806, and instructed to ensure that 'the Mission preached no more to the native people, nor distributed pamphlets, nor sent out native preachers'.[33] The following year, there was further trouble over the publication of a tract in Persian from the Mission Press and the missionaries were summoned again on 2 September 1807. They came under fire outside India as well. In an 1808 pamphlet, Major John Scott-Waring, an old Company hand and sometime political agent of Warren Hastings, thundered: '(A) gratuitous distribution of our Holy Scriptures by persons dependent upon the Company . . . should be prohibited, because it would induce the natives to believe that if we could not *persuade*, we should ultimately *compel* them to embrace Christianity.'[34]

Going West

In 1811 Chamberlain was again sent westwards, this time with a view to extending the reach of the Baptist mission beyond Digha: '(I)t was considered necessary that its operations should be extended, in order that translations already made of the Scriptures into the languages of the

---

[33] Ibid. [34] Scott-Waring, *Letter to the Rev. John Owen*, 50.

Upper Provinces, might be distributed and improved.'[35] Accordingly, Chamberlain set off towards Agra in January 1812 by boat, accompanied by one Brother Peacock. As the boat made its way through the vast Gangetic plain towards Agra, a whole new linguistic and geographical world opened up before Chamberlain's eyes:

> -28 Feb. 1811. *On the Ganges near Patna.* We are now advancing into Hindoostan, where I find a language prevailing in some respects very strange to me. ... At Monghyr, I was engaged one whole day of preaching to crowds of people ... and numbers followed me to the boat, which lay at a great distance from the bazar, for books and tracts. Upwards of thirty books and one hundred tracts were given away.[36]
>
> -25 April 1811. *On the Jumna, near Kalpee.* ... people began to come to the boat to inquire after the new book ... and we were crowded till the evening, when I stood by the side of the river, and preached to hundreds of people, giving away tracts and parts of the New Testament. ... Three Sunscrit New Testaments, and considerably more than fifty parts of the New Testament, were sent abroad, and some hundreds of tracts.
>
> -31 May 1811. *Agra.* I hope you will send me the remainder of the Hindoostanee New Testament; and if you could get a few more Christian Gospels, they would be very acceptable, as the Mussulmans and many Hindoos read nothing but Persian. But above all, we want English Bibles. I hope that you will send up a store as soon as possible, 50 at least, and as many other books as you can spare. English books are in demand, and not to be obtained.

It is clear that regardless of the obstacles placed by the Company, the mission was determined to extend its sphere of influence all the way to the

---

[35] Yates, *John Chamberlain*, 256. [36] Ibid., 268.

erstwhile Mughal seats of power in Agra and Delhi. In Chamberlain (who lost all three daughters in the summer of 1811), they found someone who was linguistically gifted and willing to suffer the rigours of life on the road. Unfortunately, he was also a bit of a loose cannon and soon got into trouble in Agra. N. B. Edmonstone, the secretary to government, fired off an angry letter to Marshman, accusing Chamberlain of attempting to convert the inhabitants 'by declamatory harangues, and Challenges to Controversy on points of Religious Faith in publicly reviling the Koraun, and the Shasters and the Religious Ceremonies of the Hindoos, and in diffusing tracts obnoxious to the religions of the Country'.[37]

On 11 March 1812, a devastating fire engulfed the printing office, destroying many manuscripts, much of the standing type and press furniture. The printing presses, the punches and the matrices were however largely untouched and this enabled the missionaries to recover quickly. Donations were raised from Britain and America, and the missionaries were able to file a new memoir in June. Understandably, there was not a great deal to report, but the missionaries used the opportunity to review the impact of the translation on their intended readerships. For instance, the report quotes a correspondent from Odisha, John Peter, as writing on 20 December 1811:

> I have engaged nine persons to read the Orissa Scriptures, for the purpose of ascertaining the character of the translation; and I have read them to many others. They all declare, this is the Orissa language; though some say, there are some Sungskrit words in it. Concerning the Marathi translation, an unnamed gentleman is quoted as writing to William Ward: '[T]he style and language of the Mahratta new testament are well understood and much commended ... Mahadeo, to whom I gave a new testament, has read it nearly twice through, and is greatly interested in its contents. Krishna has read the new testament through once, and

[37] Edmonstone to Marshman, 13 September 1811, Baptist Mission Society archives, MSS, IN/17.

he seems interested equally with Mahadeo. Bhuwanee is
reading the new testament through a second time, and
seems rather more warmly attached to it than the other
two. Narayuna, a youth, is reading the new testament
a second time to his mother and others of his family.'[38]

Here, and elsewhere, there are indications of the missionaries trying to
piece together a tally of reader responses. In many cases, such readers
served as beta-testers for a translation in progress or, occasionally, active
collaborators in translating. Among the early readers, some were to become
preachers themselves, such as the duo of Mahadeo and Narayuna in the
aforementioned passage. In May 1813, the missionary W. Moxon was able
to report from Nagpur that the two 'went to the northward on a survey, read
the Gospel in most of the villages; in one, they left a Testament and some
tracts'.[39]

But the most detailed reckoning of the 'gratuitous distribution' of Bibles
is to be found in the 'Circular Letters' which the missionaries printed at
regular intervals, comprising letters, reports and journals from the field. In
volume six of 1813, a list of Bibles and tracts distributed from Serampore for
the first quarter of 1813 is provided, giving us a fascinating real-time
glimpse of the actual number of books out for circulation (the two figures
are for books and tracts respectively being carried by the itinerant):[40]

Taken for distribution by Krishna on his journey through	206;
Assam	1182
Sent to brother W. Carey, junior, at Cutwa	14; 160
To the chapel for distribution in Calcutta, &c	37; 314
To Brother Gordon at the jail	6; 25
By a friend for distribution in Benares	60
To Brother Thompson at Patna	147; 403
Distributed at Trivenee at a late Hindu festival	12
Distributed by Brother Thomas and native brethren locally	36; 5371

---

[38] 'Memoir Relative to Translations', 524. [39] *Monthly Circular Letters*, 112.
[40] Ibid., 87–8.

Sent with Brother Robinson to Java	0; 80
Sent to Brother D'Cruz at Malda	0; 20
To Ceylon	0; 200
To the Upper Provinces	0; 25

What emerges from the above is a veritable map of the 'missionary nation' at work, ramifying from Serampore to the Upper Provinces in the west, Ceylon in the south, Assam in the north-east and Java in the south-east. The testaments and books appear to have been distributed in the immediate hinterland, while the more portable tracts were sent out to distant locations such as Ceylon and Java. One literally 'captive' readership was the jail inmates in Calcutta. But there is little corresponding data about how these books were used, or read, by their intended audience. And even when there is such data, they are filtered through a missionary sensibility. It is in vain that the book historian looks for such memorials and accounts by the readers themselves, which are also not part of the missionary discourse. By and large, the practice of sowing tracts broadcast does not seem to have yielded any worthwhile returns in terms of conversion. The eagerness with which the tracts were reportedly received may simply have been out of novelty, or even for the repurposing of the paper. Therefore, it is not surprising that occasional reports of the acceptance of the Bible were seized upon with great avidity in the missionary press. In one report, for instance, we have:

> . . . the Hindee version has been sought and eagerly read in Orissa, and Malda, at Patna, and even as far as Agra, which embraces a circuit of more than a thousand miles. It seems also to have been read with interest around us; copies having been requested by natives of various parts of India frequenting or residing in Calcutta or its neighbourhood. Among others, several from a battalion of sepoys stationed within a few miles of us, but among whom we have never been, have repeatedly come to Serampore soliciting copies of this version; and in some instances,

> they have afterwards employed us to bind them at their
> own expense.[41]

We have this account, for example, from 1817, when the mission extended its operations to Dacca, in eastern Bengal:

> Seventeen years after, when the mission extended to the old
> capital of Dacca, there were found several villages of
> Hindoo-born peasants who had given up idol-worship,
> were renowned for their truthfulness, and, as searching for
> a true teacher come from God, called themselves 'Satya-
> gooroos'. They traced their new faith to a much-worn book
> kept in a wooden box in one of their villages. No one could
> say whence it had come; all they knew was that they had
> possessed it for many years. It was Carey's first Bengali
> version of the New Testament.[42]

But perhaps the most vivid account of such encounters came from Chamberlain's two trips into the Gangetic plain, which yielded vignettes of the individual reader as well as communities. Prominent among the former was Paramanand, later christened Anund Messeh, and the centre of one of the most dramatic and oft-reported textual encounters of the time.[43] In 1813, Chamberlain had found himself ordered upcountry once again, to a place where he was expected to stay out of trouble. This place was Sirdhana, a town approximately forty miles from Delhi and the seat of the Begum Sumroo, an ally of the British. Chamberlain reprised his river journey of a year ago, and then proceeded variously by horse, elephant, buggy and palanquin, and reached Sirdhana at the height of the north Indian summer on 8 May 1813. In a letter dated the following day, Chamberlain wrote:

> It is a painful circumstance that I have not a single copy of
> the Scriptures in any language of the country to present to

[41] Ibid. [42] Smith, *William Carey*, 255.
[43] For a detailed account, see Gupta, 'What Really Happened'.

her Highness. Nothing would have pleased her more than
a copy of Sebastiani's Gospels in Persian. Mr Martyn's
Gospel of St Matthew has been presented to her by Major
Sherwood. I shall want as many of Martyn's Gospels and
Sebastiani's as you can send, five more Arabic Bibles, or ten,
if you can spare them, and forty or fiftee of your Hindee
Gospels.[44]

The high point of Chamberlain's career in north India occurred in
April 1814, when he proceeded to the temple town of Hurdwar
(Haridwar), seat of Hindu pilgrimage fair the Kumbh Mela. While
a 'purna' or a total Kumbh Mela is held every twelve years, an 'arddh'-
Kumbh or half a Kumbh is held every six years. Chamberlain attended one
of the 'ardh' or half Kumbhs, and his journal entry of 23 April 1814 provides
a vivid account of the proceedings:

It is a week since I returned home from Hurdwar, where we
remained fourteen days . . . I took all the books I had for
distribution: but amongst the immense multitudes assembled
there, all were very few indeed; ten times the number might
have been sent abroad with ease: for days we had but one
Gospel of Matthew in Hindee, and not one in Bengalee left.
It was astonishing to see the multitudes of the Shikhs; they
literally overwhelmed the people of Hindoostan, and it was
very pleasing to find so many of them who could read. Five
thousand of the Gospels would scarcely have sufficed them
all. One Raja came with 30,000 followers, when we had not
a book to give them. . . . Every evening I was surrounded
with a very large congregation, to which I preached till
dusk; from the beginning to the ending, two or three
hours. . . . I preached in the Hinduwee, which all appeared
to understand, both Bengalees and Hindoostanees. I found it
difficult to understand the Shikhs, but I believe I should be

---

[44] Yates, *John Chamberlain*, 328.

able in a short period to preach to them in their own language, were I to be called to it. Had I had some Pushtoo and Persian Gospels, I should have been able to have sent some into Persia and Candahar.[45]

Some of the Bibles that Chamberlain distributed at the fair would resurface three years later in May 1817, in the possession of a group of villagers under a tree outside Delhi. Those familiar with Homi Bhabha's essay[46] on the subject will be aware of how the reports of the gathering emanated from a 'native catechist' Anund Messeh. What Bhabha's essay does not reveal is the route by which those books reached the outskirts of Delhi, how Anund Messeh, who had been born as Parmanand in a village near Delhi, came to be a catechist, and who the group of villagers were (they turned out to be the Saadhs, a monotheistic Hindu sect). From Chamberlain's accounts, we learn of how he met Parmanand and how the two collaborated on the translation of the New Testament into the Braj-Bhasha. As I have argued elsewhere, Anund Messeh's somewhat breathless account of a group of villagers who had taken the 'English book' into their lives may have been crafted strategically for missionary ears. After the initial excitement in the missionary press about the newly discovered faithful, subsequent references were markedly less jubilant. Consider, for example, this extract from the *Missionary Register* of 1819:

Three or four years ago, (Anund heard) . . . a copy or two of the Serampore Translation of some of the Gospels were brought from Hurdwar, by some of their persuasion, who had visited the Fair. Of the spirit and proper meaning of these books, however, they knew very little; till, about ten months ago, some passages were read to them and explained by Anund Messeeh. . . . At first, a good deal of superstitious apprehension deterred them from meddling with religious matters . . . As they have, however, obtained further information, their prejudices are considerably abated; so much

[45] Ibid., 347–8. [46] Bhabha, 'Signs Taken for Wonders'.

> so, indeed, that they are very ready to receive and to use our
> books, and to listen to Anund's comments. ... As Anund
> has been repeatedly cautioned, not to let his warm imagina-
> tion delude him into any exaggerated representations of
> what he may deem worth observing and communicating,
> I have no hesitation in believing this statement.[47]

With the Anund Messeh episode, missionary aspirations about the reception and acceptance of the Bible in India may have reached a kind of impasse. Despite the Saadhs eagerly receiving tracts at the Hurdwar fair, and carrying them around three years later, they did not prove to be an easy graft for Christianity, and frustrated the missionary agenda by entering into a wholly material – and perhaps materialistic – relationship with the printed book. In such rare cases where the Bible was cherished out of piety, its value stemmed from its status as a tangible object, and not from the text it propagated. Thus, the value attached by the 'Satya-Gooroos' near Dacca was not to the letter of the New Testament but to the battered Serampore first edition kept inside a wooden box and worshipped.

Many of these apprehensions came to a head at the missionary con-
ference of September 1855, where more than one respondent acknowledged that the free distribution of tracts had been a largely futile exercise. Rev. James Long, ethnographer and the first bibliographer of the Bengali book, held that 'gratuitous distribution ... had done little to either promote Christianity' and that 'natives are not likely to value much what has cost them nothing'.[48] He went so far as to claim the education imparted through the vernacular schools in Bengal was 'not enough to enable a native to read the Bible intelligently'.[49] Long was of the opinion that Christian literature in the vernaculars – at least in Bengali – had failed as the education policy of the day favoured education in English over education in the vernacular, thereby diminishing the latter. This was part of a larger argument Long was making at that point about the unsuitability of education in English for the peasantry,[50] and how the post-1835 shift towards English benefitted only the

---

[47] 'Account of the Saadhs', 91. [48] Long, 'Vernacular Christian Literature', 130.
[49] Ibid., 127. [50] Oddie, *James Long of Bengal*, 41–2.

urban elite and intelligentsia. He was convinced that neither the government, nor the zamindars and the 'rich natives', or the English-educated elite
would carry out 'real diffusion of knowledge among the masses'. More
interestingly, Long admitted that the recent boom in Bengali letters ('these
have had a circulation of probably not less than twenty million copies')
owed nothing to missionary efforts: 'Over all these how little influence have
Christians had! Our English teaching, valuable as it is for a certain *class*, has
had little effect on the *national literature;* it has been an attempt to blend oil
and water.'[51]

The Trail of Textbooks

There is a measure of irony in this, as the missionaries had been more than
active participants in the framing of the very curricula that Long was now
deploring. From the second decade of the nineteenth century, the missionaries were beginning to get involved more openly in the production of
pedagogical material, especially for the schools that had been set up in the
Hooghly district. This can be dated from the arrival of Robert May of the
London Missionary Society in August 1812. Narrowly escaping being
arrested and deported by the East India Company, May found safe haven
in Serampore and proceeded to set up a cluster of schools in nearby
Chinsurah the following year. That year, Carey proposed a curricular
model based on the following five textbooks: arithmetic, geography,
a chronological epitome of general history, 'a selection from their own
books' and a 'selection of scripture ethics'.[52] Carey's note also coincided
with the Charter Act of 1813, which renewed the charter of the East India
Company for another twenty years and resulted, among other things, in
a greater degree of congruence between missionary and government
impulses, particularly in education.

It is in this sector, I argue, where missionary literature had a greater and
more meaningful impact on the spread of print into the hinterland. This was
not carried out directly as part of the mission's activities but through the
CSBS), which had been set up in 1817 to publish school textbooks. Formed

[51] Long, 'Vernacular Christian Literature', 124–5.
[52] 'First Report of the Calcutta School-Book Society', 148–50.

through what N. L. Basak calls an 'Europeo-Native' impulse, the CSBS was one of several set up during this period for the same purpose, such as the Calcutta School Society (1818), the Dacca and Moorshidabad School Societies (1818 and 1819 respectively), the Madras School Society (1820) and the Bombay Native School & School Book Society (1820).[53] Based in Calcutta, it was effectively the first body that was successful in selling books out of Calcutta on a sustainable model. The first two of the society's publications were books on arithmetic, authored by the Rev. May and Rev. Harle respectively. May's *Ganita*, published in 1818, ran into four editions by 1852, with the first three editions having a cumulative print run of 4,000. The other textbook was Rev. J. Harle's *Ganitanka: Harle's Arithmetic*, which was also a steady seller, and went into five editions by 1846. Rev. W. H. Pearce's *Bhugol brittanta*, a textbook of geography, was printed in a first edition of 2,000: according to Long, a total of 9,000 copies had been sold up to 1846. The highest print runs were achieved by the two parts of Radhakanta Deb's *Nitikatha*, or 'Fables in the Bengalee Language', with 5,000 and 4,000 copies respectively. The other subjects in which the Society printed were astronomy, geography, primers, spelling books, moral tales, maps and so on.

How did these books reach the intended readers? The first attempt to do so was at the behest of Radhakanta Deb, a member of the CSBS's managing committee, who 'offered to make his house the Depository of the publications it wished to introduce, and to distribute them at certain periods to Schoolmasters in the neighbourhood'.[54] Amalendu De reports that Deb was in charge of nearly 900 students in forty-two *pathshalas* or primary schools in the north Calcutta area, and distributed CSBS textbooks to the teachers of the schools. The success of the project resulted in the division of Calcutta into four divisions, and four society members were put in charge of distribution.[55] Requests from district towns and villages soon began to pour in: Capt. Stewart wrote from Contai (Kanthi) in May 1819 asking for the Society's books to be distributed among the local population, while Rev. Thomson reported from Bankura: 'At the Burdwan schools, the tables

[53] Basak, 'Calcutta School Book Society', 31.   [54] 'Second Report', 87.
[55] De, 'Text-Books in Bengali', 74.

and essays, and books of fables printed by the Society, are in constant use. Twelve schools are established in the villages around Burdwan, each of them containing on an average one hundred boys, and in all of them the use of the Society's books have been attended with the best effects.'[56]

Buoyed by its early success, the society decided to set up a number of ancillary bodies, such as the Calcutta School Society and the Dacca and Moorshidabad societies. One of the proposed arrangements was to use the Board of Revenue, in their capacity as Court of Wards, to supply books to young people under their charge. At the same time, it was not always possible for the Society to reach schools in the hinterland. As De points out, not too many *pathshalas* outside Calcutta were under European control; then the cost of sending books outside the city was often prohibitive.[57] By the early 1830s, the channels for distribution became more varied. In a report tabled by a committee in the House of Commons, it was noted that 'the different institutions of Calcutta and its neighbourhood have continued ... to receive supplies from the stores at half the cost price; and the applications for the books from the Upper Provinces are upon the increase'. The following bodies were now involved in the distribution of the Society's books: the general Committee of Public Instruction, the Hindoo College, the School Society, the European schools, several European regimental schools and missionary associations. It was reported that there was a 'regular demand' for such books among 'native booksellers'. The retail shop near Hindoo College, the first of its kind, however, had to be closed following high overheads and a recent burglary![58]

But there was another factor that facilitated the rapid spread of textbooks in the districts. This was the near-simultaneous rise of the Bengali-language periodical press from Calcutta. In April and May of 1818, the Serampore missionaries launched the first-ever Bengali periodical and the first-ever Bengali newspaper, the *Dig-darshan* and the *Samachar darpan* respectively. This was followed by the *Sambad kaumudi* (December 1821), the *Samachar chandrika* (March 1822), the *Bamgadut* (May 1829), the *Sambad prabhakar* (January 1831), the *Jnananweshan* (June 1831), the *Sambad purnochandraday*

[56] 'Second Report', 80. [57] De, 'Text-Books in Bengali', 74.

[58] 'Appendix I, Education of Natives', 256.

(June 1835) and the *Sambad bhaskar* (March 1839). Among others things, they reported extensively on the Society's activities, the setting up of new schools, and the publication of new books. Though their circulation numbers were not huge, together they constituted a considerable body of print circulating on at least a weekly basis. More importantly, their sustained reporting on education and letters went a long way in socialising both print and the new pedagogy that was being experimented.

The Rise of English

At the time of the founding of the CSBS, Bengali was the most preferred among the Society's choice of languages for publication. But as early as 1819, the Society had observed:

> The English language possesses strong claims to the early notice of this Institution. Though it were unreasonable to expect that it can ever become the vernacular language in the country, it ought certainly to be considered as an important instrument for the diffusion of useful knowledge, as it will probably . . . become the learned language in India. As far as we can open to the Natives the presence of the English language, so far we put them in the possession of true knowledge, Natives learned in the English may become highly useful instructors of their fellow countrymen.[59]

One may see here the blueprint for the project that would come to fruition a decade and a half later in 1835, with T. B. Macaulay's 'Minute on Education'. In the twenty-fifth paragraph of that minute, Macaulay had noted that while Arabic and Sanskrit books were hardly selling, 'the School Book Society is selling seven or eight thousand English volumes every year, and not only pays the expenses of printing but realizes a profit of twenty per cent on its outlay'.[60] This is confirmed the following year in the Society's report

---

[59] 'The Second Report', 10.   [60] 'Minute by the Hon'ble T. B. Macaulay'.

Our language has taken deep root in the seats of the four
Presidencies, Calcutta, Allahabad, Madras, Bombay; and in
the following places in Hindustan, viz., Ludiana, Meerut,
Agra, Delhi, Kotah, Futtephur, Lukhnow, Gorukhpur,
Benaras, Patna, Berhampur, Bauleah, Chhota Nagpur,
Dhaka, Chitagong, Munipur, and several other stations. It
is now beginning to spread in some parts of Ceylon, Orissa,
Burmah, and Assam.[61]

Increased sales of the Society's books were reported from the depositories at Calcutta and Cawnpore (Kanpur), as well as the setting up of new
depositories at Lukhnow, Agra and Ludiana. Of the 52,423 copies of books
sold in the two years 1834 and 1835, as many as 31,649 were in English,
followed by Bengali at 5,764, Hindi at 4,171, and Hindustani at 3,384.
A curious category, 'Anglo-Asiatic', accounted for 4,252 copies. These
were books of Indian languages in roman script, an initiative mooted by
Charles Trevelyan in 1834 in order to bypass the necessity of using different
typefaces for different languages. Four years later, in 1852, the Society was
able to report an almost 100% increase in its sales.

The tally in Table 1 is fascinating for a number of reasons, which lie
beyond the remit of the study (the resurgence of romanised books, the
fading of Arabic and Persian and experiments with the Santali language),
but what is most noticeable is the proliferation of books in the English
language by the mid-century, a trend that would continue through the 1850s
(in 1855, the number of English books sold would be more than double the
total of Bengali books). The rise in the number of English books was
mirrored by a corresponding rise in 'English schools' both in Calcutta
and the districts, a phenomenon enthusiastically reported upon by the
periodical press. While the early schools were all within the city limits of
Calcutta, the early 1830s saw the setting up of 'branch' schools in the
districts. A chief impulse behind such schools was the Rev. Alexander
Duff, the first overseas missionary of the Church of Scotland. Duff arrived
in Calcutta in 1830, and following the success of the General Assembly

[61] 'Calcutta School Book Society', 172.

Table 1 Abstract of the books issued from the CSBS Depository from 1 Jan. 1848, to 31 Dec. 1851[62]

	1848	1849	1850	1851	Total
English	12,484	14,399	14,311	24,572	65,766
Anglo-Asiatic	512	499	2,229	9,000	12,240
Sanscrit	270	186	102	285	843
Bengali	13,063	13,914	11,759	19,389	58,125
Uriya	2	3	22	68	95
Santal	0	0	1,502	11	1,513
Hindui	1,129	1683	2,000	3,532	8,344
Arabic	32	2	12	15	61
Persian	323	112	1,479	262	2,176
Urdu	2,384	1,996	1,716	3,803	9,899

Institution in Calcutta, was invited to set up similar schools outside the city.[63] In 1832, the first such school was established at Taki, about fifty miles east of Calcutta. In November 1834, an English school was set up in Midnapore (Medinipur) through a private initiative before being made over to the government in 1835. In 1836, the *Calcutta Courier* reported the setting up of a school near Barrackpur, followed by schools in Shantipur, Andul, Baranagar, Maheshpur, Barasat, Telenipara and Murshidabad over 1837–40.[64] These schools all offered English in their curricula and were mostly set up through local philanthropy and subscriptions. Many more such schools would come up in the next decades, fuelling the need for more books in the classroom.

All through this, the Society continued to grapple with ways of making its publications widely available in the hinterland. The thirteenth report of the Society in 1845 listed as many as twenty-five 'mofussil depositories' that had been set up, and noted that however distant the station, the price of the

[62] *Fifteenth Report*, 16. [63] Kocchar, *English Education in India*. [64] Ibid., 66–81.

books was the same as that in Calcutta.[65] In two years' time, the list had
dwindled to seventeen, chiefly owing to the setting up of a Government
Book Agency and a Book Agent in Calcutta, through which books for
schools and colleges were now routed.[66] But following the abolition of the
Government Book Agency in 1856, the Society fell back on the tried and
tested system of mofussil depositories, with a little help from Hodgson
Pratt, the inspector of schools for southern Bengal. Pratt proposed a system
of agents and sub-agents in interior locations, which may be regarded as
forerunners of the modern distribution system for print. In the nineteenth
report of the committee in 1856, it was proposed that some sub-inspectors of
schools be employed as agents, who in turn could supply local pedlars. The
same year, this system was explained by Hodgson Pratt:

> Finding that my previous attempts to establish Bookshops
> and Book Agencies in the towns and villages of the interior
> had not succeeded ... other measures have been adopted,
> which consist in appointing the Sub-Inspectors to be Agents
> of the Society, with power to supply books on credit to the
> subordinate Agents in the interior. ... They receive
> 10 per cent ... on condition of not charging more to their
> customers than the retail price fixed by the School Book
> Society, and of not selling any books which have not been
> previously approved. The object of these mofussil agencies
> is two-fold, *viz.*, to place within the reach of the native public
> good and useful books at low prices, and to enable our new
> Schools to obtain class-books easily and cheaply.[67]

It may seem curious for a government official to take such interest in the
retail trade of books, but we have to remember that these were early days
for the textbooks market, and competition had not become as cutthroat as it
would be two decades on. As the textbooks market became lucrative and
local publishers faced stiff challenges from the likes of Macmillan and

---

[65] *Fifteenth Report*, 17. [66] *Fourteenth Report*, 15.
[67] 'Report of the Director of Public Instruction', 20.

Oxford University Press towards the end of the nineteenth century, government would tend to frown upon school inspectors getting involved in the textbooks trade, especially as the DPI (director of public instruction) would also be the titular head of the textbook committees. In the 1850s, it was still possible for the likes of a Hodgson Pratt to take a pro bono interest in the dispersion of textbooks. By the mid-1860s, the system of agency had taken extensive roots not just in Bengal, but all over India. In the annual report of 1867–68, the list of agents ran to nearly six pages of print. "The Agents in Bengal are chiefly School-masters and Deputy Inspectors in the Government Education Department; those in the North Western Provinces, are either missionaries themselves, or persons under their immediate superintendence',[68] the report observed.

Finally, what of the intended reader of the textbooks, the students themselves? Accounts by school-going children of their readings are scarce, but such as those exist are revealing. Take the instance of Akshaychandra Sarkar, born in 1846 in Chinsurah. Both father (Gangacharan) and son were students of Hooghly College, one of the first colleges to set up outside Calcutta, in 1836. By the age of ten, the precocious Akshaychandra had read the annuals of the periodical *Sambad prabhakar*, the *Annadamangal*, Bengali primers, Akshaychandra Dutta's work on natural sciences, and Bengali adaptations of the *Arabian Nights*, Shakespeare and *Paul et Virginie*. He had read little of English other than some spelling books and readers, but had read Pearson's geography and Yeats's physics in Bengali translation.[69] Admittedly, Akshaychandra – who was methodically mentored in his reading by his father – was not your average school-goer, but his list does indicate the reach of both the commercial as well as the textbooks market into the hinterland by the mid-century. The linguist Shyamacharan Gangopadhyay, born eight years before Akshaychandra in 1838, learnt to read English in a remote village school in Garalgacha village near Serampore in the early 1840s.[70]

---

[68] *Twenty-Fifth Report*, 24–30.

[69] Akshaychandra Sarkar, 'Pita putra', quoted in Brajendranath, *SSK no.* 39, 6.

[70] Sastri, *Rachana-sangraha*, vol. 2, 50.

But perhaps the most engaging account of reading came from the historian and educationist Sibnath Sastri (b. 1847). Sastri went to a village school in Majilpur thirty miles south of Calcutta where he recalls reading the CSBS's *Barnamala* and the Bengali primer of Madanmohan Tarkalankar.[71] A stray dog was named Robert[72] after a character from the *First Book of Reading*, a textbook which was imported by the CSBS from Messrs. W. and R. Chambers of Edinburgh.[73] But what is most remarkable is how Sastri's mother Golokmani took to reading. Sastri's father had been a student of Sanskrit College in Calcutta, and had come under the spell of Ishwarchandra Bidyasagar.[74] He taught his wife to read and young Sibnath soon saw his mother reading *Annadmangal,* the *Ramayana,* the *Mahabharata* and *Romeo and Juliet.* The last-named would probably have been the 1848 translation by Gurudas Hajra from Charles Lamb's *Tales of Shakespeare*, the first-ever Bengali adaptation from Shakespeare. The books roused curiosity in a young widow who lived next door, and she would ask the boy Sastri to teach her letters[75]. Clearly, print was no longer confined to classrooms in the city and had found a way into the household.

---

[71] Sastri, *Atmacharit*, 25.   [72] Ibid., 58.   [73] *Twentieth Report*, 5.

[74] The figure of Ishwarchandra Bidyasagar – reformer, educationist, print pioneer, publisher and philanthropist – is unavoidable in any discussion on print in colonial Bengal. Among others, he was responsible for standardising the Bengali type-case, and easily the most successful publisher of his time. His Sanskrit Press virtually cornered the market for textbooks publishing in the mid-nineteenth century.

[75] Sastri, *Atmacharit*, 29.

2 Out of Calcutta

In this chapter, I propose to look at specific nodes of printing in Calcutta's hinterland, and the flows of people, skills and materials that sustained them. Owing to limitations of space, this will be a preliminary sketch, with the choice of locales likewise constrained. While this chapter cannot do full justice to the variety of printing models that originated outside the metropolis, it hopes to draw attention to some of the key features of such models. In doing so, I hope to show how many of these nascent nodes of printing were able to fashion alternative ecosystems of print production and consumption.

It is not surprising that given the elaborate network at their disposal, the missionaries should have been among the first to set up printing presses in the hinterland. In the case of eastern India, one thinks of locations such as Chinsurah, Cuttack, Midnapore, Sibsagar and so on, where the missionaries set up presses with varying degree of success. These were necessitated, in the first place, to reduce dependence on parent centres in Serampore and Calcutta. As Graham Shaw points out in his account of early Odia printing, 'it became more and more inconvenient and irksome to send all materials for printing three hundred miles or more to Serampore or Calcutta'.[76] This impulse led to the setting up of the Orissa Mission Press in Cuttack in 1838, and to the beginning of printing in Odisha. Likewise, missionaries Nathan Brown and Oliver Cutter endured an arduous journey from Calcutta with a printing press in tow to set up the first printing establishment in Assam at Sibsagar in 1846.

But the trajectory of such a press set up by indigenous initiative was completely different. As we have seen from the instance of Gangakishore, it was possible for an enterprising printer to set up a press in a distant village, and even run a business from there. But Gangakishore's case was exceptional. He had already made a name and fortune for himself in the city, and was more or less the only player in the field. By the mid-1820s, a clutch of half-a-dozen indigenous printers had set up shop in Calcutta, but by then Gangakishore had moved out of the city. We do not have much information

---

[76] Shaw, 'The Cuttack Mission Press', 35.

about this period of his career, but it does appear that he was able set up networks of distribution with the aid of his 'agents'. But there were good reasons why Gangakishore's model was not immediately replicable. Despite his seeming success, there was no ready market for books or periodicals outside the city. Owning books was still considered a novelty: in 1819, the *Samachar darpan* was moved to comment on the fact that 'someone who had acquired one book was now trying to acquire another'.[77] And though it continued to report with enthusiasm on the rise of the periodical press in Calcutta through the 1820s, there is no evidence that such newspapers had a sufficient subscription base even within the city. To give just one example: in 1830, the cumulative print run of thirty-three English newspapers in the city was just 2,250.[78] In any case, postal charges were an impediment to sending newspapers outside the city – even after reductions made during the governor-generalship of the liberal William Bentinck, the lowest postal charge for a newspaper was two annas.[79] Bengali-language newspapers did not fare much better either. In 1840, a report on the 'Native Press' in the *Calcutta Christian Observer* estimated that the nine regular Bengali-language news-periodicals printed in the city had a cumulative circulation of 2,231 in the city, while 319 copies were dispatched to subscribers.[80] Nevertheless, as we shall see later in the chapter, print runs – particularly of periodicals – were not always the most significant indicator of the success or failure of a paper.

In order to understand the differences and similarities between metropolitan and small town printing in Bengal, let us consider what business models were available to printers during this time, outside of missionary and government printing. In the early decades of the nineteenth century, patronage was a major source of venture capital for religious publications, especially of Hindu epics or scriptures. Such books would often be given away free, an act of piety on part of the patron or the publisher. A similar appeal to piety and tradition was made when publishers sought advance subscriptions from the wealthy for religious titles. But patronage was also forthcoming for new genres of printing such as the newspaper or the

---

[77] Brajendranath, *SSK*, vol. 1, 59.   [78] Natrajan, *Press in India*, 58–9.   [79] Ibid.
[80] 'The Calcutta Native Press', 66.

magazine, and was part of a lager project of modernisation. At the head of the project were a number of a humanist-printers led by the reformist Raja Rammohan Roy who set up the Unitarian Press in 1821 and founded periodicals in Bengali, English and Persian. The humanist model, as we will see, was particularly fruitful for the rise and growth of printing in the hinterland, and especially of the periodical press.

By the mid-century, a full-fledged book trade – governed by the rules of the market – had taken shape in the Battala area of north Calcutta, with the term 'Battala' becoming a metonym for the Calcutta book trade. There are a number of excellent studies on the Battala trade, exploring, among other things, how printers and entrepreneurs from the districts set up presses and businesses in the city. Then there was the burgeoning and extremely lucrative textbooks market, whose presses and depositories were contiguous to Battala but embodied a publishing sensibility at odds with that of Battala. Societies of arts and letters such as the Asiatic Society, the Vernacular Literature Society and of course the CSBS provided yet another business model. Finally, the rise of the reformist Brahmo movement, and conservative Hindu opposition to it, produced a considerable body of polemics, particularly in the periodical press.

None of the above was exclusive to either the city or the mofussil, and we have to be careful not to fall into the trap of simple binaries. Almost all of the above models found application in both sectors, though the scale of operations might be seen to differ. In many cases, it was easier for printers in the city to mobilise more venture capital in comparison to their country counterparts. But there were also city printers who subsisted on narrow margins and limited resources. Again, it would seem tempting to generalise that city printers and publishers were part of a group with exclusive access to the levers of financial and cultural capital. But in at least two of the nodes of district printing we will survey, there was unfettered access to such capital on part of the printer-publishers.

How then shall we measure the significance of the printing that was carried out in the hinterland? It is my suggestion that we do so by asking a number of questions which considers hinterland printing as a self-sustaining process, rather than as ancillary to the city's. What were the key features of printing in the hinterland? What conditions were necessary to make it happen? What were the financial models which sustained these presses, both in the short as well as the long run? What was the role played by the metropolis in incubating these centres, if any? Did the district presses only cater to local readers or did they also reach the city? Owing to the paucity of primary sources, and particularly printers' records, not all these questions can be answered satisfactorily. Nevertheless, even partial answers – or educated guesses – to some of these queries may be possible from the available data.

The Pre-Catalogue Period

Let us look at the available data. Here, there is a clear watershed: the 1867 Press and Registration Act – or Act XXV of the Governor-General in Council for 1867 – which made it compulsory for all printers and publishers to register every publication in British India for a sum of two rupees. Any unregistered publication was deemed to be outside the law and its publisher or printer could be punished with a two-year jail sentence and a 5,000 rupees fine. By printing the returns as a 'catalogue', issued four times a year as a supplement to its official gazette, the government of Bengal kept a record of all the books published in the province.[81] These records provide a running bibliographical tally of all books and periodicals printed over the entirety of British India till 1947, and in some cases, even later.

For books printed during the pre-1867 period, I have relied on my own bibliographical database[82] of Bengali books printed during 1801–67, as well as those by the Rev. James Long, Muntasir Mamoon, Jatindramohan Bhattacharya, M. F. Khan and so on. For periodicals, the most comprehensive resource is Brajendranath Bandypadhyay's several checklists of

---

[81] The 'Two Centuries of Indian Print' project at the British Library has made these volumes available online. In the case of Bengal, the files run to forty-four volumes from 1867 to 1954. See https://data.bl.uk/twocenturies-quarterlylists /tcq1.html?_ga=2.32171194.546189238.1626009454-541559830.1609225622.

[82] See https://granthsouthasia.wordpress.*com*/sct/. The database lists roughly 2,500 Bengali titles during the years 1801–67. These are the list of titles still extant in the major libraries and collections, so the historical figures would be somewhat higher.

periodicals from 1818 to 1900, Binay Ghosh's multi-volume collection of articles from newspapers and periodicals, as well as Muntasir Mamoon's studies on periodicals in eastern Bengal.

Let us begin with some numerical snapshots of printing in Bengali. Table 2 shows a list of the number of Bengali titles printed from presses outside Calcutta between 1819 and 1867. The dates next to the place-name indicates the year of publication of the first title. I must point out that these are not exact figures, but only indicative ones, with an error margin of 5 per cent. This is largely owing to the fact that quite a few of the imprints published during this period are no longer extant. The figures in the list

Table 2 Bengali books printed in presses outside Calcutta: 1819–67

Place of printing	Year of first publication	No. of titles till 1867
Dacca	1856	31
Serampore*	1854: Tamohar Press	18
Serampore	1846: Chandroday Press	13
Burdwan	1858: Satyaprakash Press et al.	15
Chinsurah	1819: School Press; 1846	6
Sibsagar	1850: American Baptist Press	1
Murshidabad-Berhampore	1864	5
Mymsensingh	1866	3
Rungpore	1860	3
Hooghly	1862: Budhoday Press	7
Krishnanagar	1863: Adhyabasay Press	3
Jessore	1867	1
Rajshahi	1867	1

* *The output of the Mission Press at Serampore has not been considered here*

below are based on books that are still extant in the major libraries and depositories.

Table 3 is a list of the number of Bengali periodicals and newspapers printed outside Calcutta, between 1818 and 1867, in order of appearance.

On the evidence of the above figures, several trends are visible. It is evident from both tallies that both books and periodicals publishing in the districts begin to take off from roughly the 1850s. Dacca, the leading city in eastern Bengal, was the most active in both books and periodicals printing, though it was a somewhat late starter in both cases. Printing in Serampore continued where the Baptists had left off – six out of the eight periodicals it tallied were missionary initiatives, with local notables joining in at a later stage. Murshidabad and Rungpore were early starters in the field of periodicals, but did not show similar activity in terms of books. Overall, periodical printing seems to have been much more widespread than the printing of books. While there were nine centres outside Calcutta that printed at least more than one book, the number of places publishing and/or printing periodicals were nearly twenty.

As far as solely periodicals are concerned, there is a clear trajectory in the character of their proprietorship. Till the 1850s, most periodicals were either funded by missionaries or through the patronage of royal families or local zamindars. The next phase saw the rise of humanist-run periodicals, as well as societies and associations. The Brahmo Samaj, and the *dharma sabha* or religious societies formed in opposition to uphold traditional Hindu beliefs, enthusiastically took to the periodical to air their differences. But from the 1860s, with the entry of Dacca into the periodicals market, there is a distinct shift towards private/individual ownership, particularly in eastern Bengal. According to Muntasir Mamoon, this was not so much by choice as through necessity, as there was little or no patronage forthcoming from the landed class of eastern Bengal, who were mostly absentee landlords.[83]

It may also be seen that some of the earlier district periodicals were printed from locations at a considerable distance from Calcutta, such as in

---

[83] Mamoon, *Unish shotoke*, 115.

Table 3 Periodicals published in presses outside Calcutta: 1818–67

Place of publication	Earliest year of periodical publication	Total	Ownership
Serampore	1818	8	Missionary 6 Individual 2
Murshidabad-Berhampore	1838	6	Royal patronage 1; Individual 5
Rungpore	1847	2	Local patronage 2
Sibpur	1848	1	Royal patronage 1
Benaras	1849	4	Individual 4; 3 lithographed
Burdwan	1849	4	Individual 2; Royal patronage 1; society 1
Konnagar	1850	1	Dharma sabha 1 (a society for preserving traditional Hindu values)
Midnapore	1851	1	Government 1
Choto Jaguliya	1853	2	Citizens' group 2
Majilpur	1856	1	Local patronage 1
Uttarpara	1856	1	Individual 1
Chinsurah	1858	1	Individual 1
Dacca	1860	13	Individual 11; Society 3
Rajpur	1860	1	Unknown
Bikrampur	1860	2	Societies 2
Changaripota	1862	1	Individual 1
Jessore	1862	1	Individual 1
Kumarkhali	1863	1	Individual 1

Table 3 Cont.

Place of publication	Earliest year of periodical publication	Total	Ownership
Pabna	1864	1	Individual 1
Hooghly	1864	2	Individual 1
Rajshahi	1867	1	Individual 1

Murshidabad, Rungpore and Benaras. If one lived within a reasonable distance of Calcutta, it made more sense to print from the city where the resources and personnel for printing were more readily available. But as the distance from the city increased, it would become increasingly difficult for a publisher or an editor to depend on Calcutta printers, and the to-and-fro involved in sending copy and checking proofs. In such cases, it would make better sense to set up a printing establishment of one's own, however basic, in situ. Such choices would also determine the periodicity of a magazine or a newspaper. If the publisher was in the distant mofussil and the printer in Calcutta, then the periodical was likely to be a monthly, or at most, a fortnightly. In order to become a weekly, one would necessarily need to have the press on one's premises.

One of the curious instances of the Bengali periodical press is that of Benaras, a centre of the Bengali diaspora. In 1849, two Bengali periodicals – both edited by Umakanta Bhattacharya who had earlier edited a Calcutta periodical from 1846–49 – appeared and disappeared in the same year. This was followed by the more lasting *Kashibarta prakashika* in 1851, edited by Kashidas Mitra, who also conducted an Urdu periodical called *Aftab-e-hind*. All three periodicals were lithographed, the first two from the short-lived Bagh-o-Bahar Press founded in 1848, and the latter from the more successful Kashi Press founded in 1851 by Mitra himself. These are likely the only instances where a Bengali publication was not produced through typography. Ulrike Stark reports that the *Kashibarta*'s circulation rose from 92 to 130 in a year, while the *Aftab-e-hind* was even more successful, enjoying the 'longest life among the early regional-language papers of Benaras'.[84] The Bagh-o-Bahar Press, on the other hand, struggled throughout its short life, and was an example of the 'limitations imposed on the early development of commercial print culture by the small size and purchasing power of the literate audience'.[85]

Returns of the Raj

We have considerably more data for the post-1867 period, and data that have a more direct bearing on printing in the mofussil. In Table 4, for example, we are able to see a comparison of copyrights registered in Calcutta's 'Office of the Registrar-General of Assurances, Lower Provinces' vis-à-vis copyrights registered in the mofussil. Figures for this are available from 1868, the year after the passage of the Press and Registration Act. The source of this data are the annual reports of the Bengal administration. Among other things, the reports would provide totals of the number of print items submitted for copyright registration. These would be divided into two categories: those that were submitted to the 'office of the registrar general of assurances, Lower Province', and those that were submitted to 'Mofussil offices'. Thus, during the year 1868–69, a total of 1,092 printed items were registered at the former while 136 were registered at the latter. Nearly a decade later, in 1876–77, the figure for registrar-general's office had fallen to 1,018 while the figure at the mofussil offices had surged to 445. But what stands out most clearly from the figures is the steady rise of the percentage of titles from the mofussil: in 1868, the percentage of titles registered in the mofussil was at 11 per cent. But within a few years, the percentage share had risen to as much as 30 per cent in 1876–77 and 31 per cent in 1882–83, indicating a threefold increase in the mofussil share in just a decade-and-a-half.

The other set of figures which are available from the annual reports provide a breakdown of the places of publication within Bengal (see Table 5), from 1874–75 onwards. A tally from 1868, with slightly different categories, can be seen in the first two columns.

---

[84] Stark, *An Empire of Books*, 61.   [85] Ibid., 62.

Table 4 Registration of copyright in Calcutta and the mofussil 1868–83

	Office of the Registrar-General of Assurances, Lower Province	Mofussil offices	Per cent (%) of mofussil titles	Total
1868–69	1,092	136	11.07	1,228
1870–71	1,000	–	–	–
1872–73	880	202	18.6	1,082
1873–74	864	217	20.07	1,081
1874–75	1,008	359	26.26	1,367
1875–76	1,082	437	28.76	1,519
1876–77	1,018	445	30.41	1,463
1877–78	1,016	383	27.37	1,399
1878–79	–	–	–	1,542
1879–80	1,118	430	27.27	1,548
1881–82	–	–	–	1,407
1882–83	1,209	543	30.99	1,752

Source: Annual Reports on the Administration of Bengal
Note: Figures for 1869–70, 1871–72 and 1880–81 are missing.

Table 5 Locations of books published in the Bengal Presidency 1868–1884

1868		1874	1876	1877	1878	1879	1882	1883	1884
1,092	Calcutta	1,504	1,106	1,172	1,105	983	1,053	1,309	1,792
13	Burdwan Division	67	59	95	52	50	56	54	57
5 + 21	Presidency Division	55	76	113	82	121	136	214	113
25	Dacca Division	72	120	101	163	121	176	139	168
20	Orissa Division	56	59	39	39	41	60	34	79
	Rajshahye Division	38	51	2	1	-	2	1	32
3	Patna Division	30	40	48	41	68	68	64	120
7	Assam Division	1	1	1	-	-	-	-	-
16	Bhugulpore Division	-	-	5	3	1	-	4	-
17	Chittagong	-	-	-	-	6	17	3	29
9	TOTAL	1,823	1,512	1,576	1,486	1,391	1,568	1,822	2,390

The left-hand location labels for the 1868 column, reading down, are: Calcutta, Burdwan, Hooghly and Serampore, Dacca, Cuttack, Jessore, Mymensingh, Howrah, Alipore, Midnapore.

Source: Annual Reports on the Administration of Bengal

Given the limited span and the occasional gaps in these figures, they can convey only a broad-brush sense of printing in the hinterland over a period of three decades immediately succeeding the Press and Registration Act. There are some unmistakable trends, such as the rapid increase in both books and periodicals printing in the centres of eastern Bengal. In 1868, for example, eastern Bengal (Dacca, Mymensing, Jessore) produced 35 titles; by 1876, this figure had swelled to 100 and to 229 by 1884. Printing of books in Patna – chiefly in the Hindi and Urdu languages – multiplied threefold between 1876 and 1884. On the other hand, printing of books in divisions closer to Calcutta i.e. in Presidency and Burdwan, either stagnated or declined slightly during the 1870s and 1880s, indicating that the early spurt in printing in these regions had either plateaued or shifted back to Calcutta.

But perhaps the most significant resource, as far as the mofussil is concerned, are the weekly 'confidential' news digests titled 'Reports on Native Papers', issued in Bengal from 1874. These were compiled from the office of the 'Bengali Translator to the Government' whose first incumbent was Rev. John Robinson, and later, Rajkrishna Mukherjee and Chandra Nath Bose. These provide a detailed and scrupulously compiled weekly account of what Bengali newspapers were saying about a wide range of issues. From 1877, they also begin to report print runs of the listed periodicals. In Table 6, I have compiled a list of some of the longer-running periodicals published outside Calcutta, in a roughly chronological order, from 1877 to the end of the century. We will consider these figures in detail as we survey the locations of their printing in the following pages, as well as in the concluding section of this book.

The next section of this chapter will take a closer look at some of the newly emergent nodes of printing in the mofussil. These are Hooghly-Chinsurah, Serampore and Burdwan from the Burdwan Division; Changaripota and Kumarkhali from the Presidency Division; and Murshidabad and Rungpore from the Rajshahi Division. The highest number of nodes occur in the Burdwan Division, and in terms of chronology, they are among the first to start printing outside Calcutta.

Table 6 Print run of select newspapers in Bengal districts 1878–99

Periodical	Place of publication	Jan 1878	Jan 1881	Jan 1885	Jan 1887	Jan 1889	Jan 1891	Jan 1893	Jan 1895	Jan 1897	Jan 1899	Year of establishment and comments
Education Gazette (w)	Hooghly	1,168	745	800	825	825	885	825	950		1350	1856
Somprakash (w)	Changaripota	700	…	1,000	1,000	1,000	1,000	600	800	800	1,000	1858
Rangpur dikprakash (w)	Kakiniya, Rungpore	250	250	220	205	205	…			180	180	1860
Dhaka prakash (w)	Dacca	400	350	425	450	450	1200	2,200	2,400	2,400	2,400	March 1861
Grambarta prakashika (m)	Kumarkhali	200	175	500	200	200						1863
Hindu ranjika (w)	Baulea, Rajshahi	…	200	200	200	200	300	212	248	195	243	March 1866
Sadharani (w)	Chinsurah	516	500	500	…							Nov 1873
Grambasi (w)	Howrah						800	1,000 (f)				1873
Murshidabad hitaisi	Murshidabad								…	836	655	1893

Table 6 Cont.

Periodical	Place of publication	Jan 1878	Jan 1881	Jan 1885	Jan 1887	Jan 1889	Jan 1891	Jan 893	Jan 1895	Jan 1897	Jan 1899	Year of establishment and comments
Murshidabad patrika (w)	Berhampore	...	487	437	508	508	...	...	...			April 1872
Murshidabad pratinidhi (w)	Berhampore	...	...	...	...	...	...	...	...	200		March 1876
Pratikar (w)	Berhampore	235	275	600		600	600	609	608	603	603	March 1876; rival to above
Paridarshak (w)	Sylhet			440	450	...	450	480	480	...	...	1880
Bharat shramjibi (m)	Baranagar	4000	2700									Apr 1874
Bharat mihir (w)	Mymensingh	658	671	625	2500 (Calcutta)							Dec 1875
Bardhaman sanjivani (w)	Burdwan		296	296	302	302	302	333	310		240	1878
Behar bandhu (w, Hindi)	Bankipore, Patna	509	500					500	500	500	About 600	1873
Sansodhini (w)	Chittagong	600	600	700	800	800	...	...	...	120	120	Oct? 1879

Title							Date
Assam News (m, Sibsagar, Assamese)	450	450					Oct 1882
Prajabandhu (w) Chandernagore	900	995					
Bankura darpan Bankura (f)	230			444	420		1892
Utkal dipika (w, Cuttack, Odia)			397	450	532	450	480	400	1866

Source: Reports on Native Newspapers 1878–1899; British Library London

Note: language of periodical is Bengali unless otherwise mentioned; w: weekly; f: fortnightly; m: monthly; an ellipsis indicates that print run was not mentioned that particular month/year. A blank indicates no information about the newspaper concerned, which may indicate a temporary cessation as well.

Serampore was already a highly developed network of printing when we take up the story, while Hooghly was equally developed in terms of schools and general literacy. In Burdwan, printing was largely carried out by the royal family, resulting in a more or less closed ecosystem, of textual production. On the other hand, Murshidabad, despite its princely origins, soon developed a network on its own, creating local nodes of both book and periodicals printing. The two villages surveyed, Changaripota and Kumarkhali, were single-press nodes, powered largely by individual initiative, but nonetheless produced two of the most significant newspapers of the day. The case of Rungpore is a study in longevity, at a time when most newspapers and periodicals tended to be short-lived. Dacca, the most prominent centre of printing after Calcutta, has not been surveyed as a wealth of scholarship already exists on the subject.

~

Twin tales: Hooghly-Chinsurah

South of Burdwan, if one proceeds downriver along the western bank of the river Hooghly, one would come across five towns one after the other. First, Bandel, founded by Portuguese settlers in the sixteenth century; then Hooghly, a river port during the Mughal era and stamping ground of European colonialists of all hues; then Chinsurah, held fitfully by the Dutch till 1825; Chandernagore, one of the last French enclaves in India, given up in 1951; and finally, Serampore, a Danish outpost till 1802. Together, these constituted one of the most active hubs of first education, and then printing, in nineteenth-century Bengal. Currently, they are part of the district of Hooghly, which gets its name from the river of the same name. In the nineteenth century, however, they fell under the Burdwan Division, which comprised the following districts: Burdwan, Midnapore, Bankura, Birbhum and Howrah with Hooghly. In this section, we will consider the twin towns of Hooghly-Chinsurah as a hyphenated unit, and on occasions, popping across the river to take in the sights of Naihati.

Though the first-ever Bengali book to be printed with moveable type was printed from Hooghly in 1778, it would be another three-quarters of a century before print would return to the town. This should not surprise us, for the history of printing in colonial India is full of such false starts and aborted attempts. Nathaniel Brassey Halhed's *A Grammar of the Bengal Language* was printed in Hooghly from a press belonging to John Andrews which then shifted to Calcutta. Then there was a lull till the Baptists fortuitously arrived in Serampore. Along with printing, the Baptists became involved in setting up primary schools in the area. In 1813, the Rev. Robert May set up a cluster of primary schools in Chinsurah. He was later joined by the Rev. Pearson who set up Hooghly's second printing press in 1819, the School Press, under the patronage of the newly set-up Calcutta School Society. The press printed some slim volumes in 1819, but soon shifted to Calcutta.

But the Chinsurah schools were to be indirect catalyst behind the first concerted attempt to print pedagogical books in Bengal, in the form of the CSBS. This was set up in 1817 to provide textbooks necessitated by the extension of the school system in Chinsurah. As we have seen in Chapter 1, such books were issued by Calcutta presses and there were no attempts to set up printing establishments in Hooghly itself. One reason for this would have been the proximity of Calcutta, a quick boat-ride away. The other was the existing of a flourishing centre of printing and publishing in neighbouring Serampore. Nevertheless, it is somewhat surprising that the second innings of Hooghly's printing would begin over three decades later, in 1861, with the educationist and writer Bhudeb Mukhopadhyay setting up the Budhoday Press, with Kashinath Bhattacharya as printer.

The impulse that led to the setting-up of the Budhoday Press could be traced to a new institution in Bengal – the Vernacular Normal School – intended for the training of teachers. The first three normal schools in Bengal were set up in the 1850s, in Calcutta, Dacca and Hooghly. The Hooghly normal school was set up in 1856 and Bhudeb – who was then in the employ of the Department of Public Instruction (DPI) – was appointed its first principal. Bhudeb was part of a group of humanists and educators in mid-nineteenth-century Bengal who also made printing an integral part of their curriculum of social reform and education. The line of humanist printers began with Raja Rammohan Roy, and continued with Ishwarchandra Bidyasagar, Bankimchandra Chattyopadhyay and the like. But what was distinctive about the careers of both Bidyasagar and Bhudeb was their close association with the DPI. Parna Sengupta points out how following the 'Wood's Despatch' of 1854, there was a recognition that the *bhadralok* or educated middle-class community had to be co-opted in the extension of vernacular education.[86] As we have seen in the last chapter, the ecosystem of primary education in Bengal had resulted in a demand for education in English; but the popularity of 'Anglo-Vernacular' schools, especially among the *bhadralok*, showed that the modernisation of the vernacular was no less an important object.[87] As Swapan Chakravorty points out, the mid-nineteenth-century world of Bengali letters was the site of an intense debate about the language of Bengali prose which cannot be understood solely in terms of linguistic registers. Among others, he draws our attention to the 'imperfect fit between colonial, missionary and native projects of regularising the vernacular for printed public discourse'[88] as one of the key narratives of this period.

It is in this context that Bhudeb's writing of pedagogical material, and their subsequent publication, assume significance. Soon after Bhudeb's appointment, the Rev. Long noted with approval that the 'principal ... gives regular lecture in the vernacular, on scientific and historical subjects; the pupil takes notes, and this leads to the production of books. ... The living teacher creates the demand for books, and provides the means for supplying it.'[89] These books were initially published from the Sucharu Press in Calcutta but in 1862, Bhudeb, along with his associate Ramgati Nyayratna decided to buy a press and pooled together a sum of Rs 1,000 for the purpose. An element of whimsy accompanied the setting-up of the press – the name of the press was designated as Budhoday because the press machinery was set up on a Wednesday (Budh being Bengali for Wednesday). Then, when the type for the press was being distributed in

---

[86] Sengupta, *Pedagogy for Religion*, 34–5. [87] Ibid.

[88] Chakravorty, 'Purity and Print', 203.

[89] Long, *Records of the Bengal Government*, liv.

cases, Bhudeb invited his students to imagine the type as molecules, and compose a line of type blindfolded.[90]

In its early years the Budhoday Press published primarily Bengali pedagogical material in history and natural philosophy, authored chiefly by Bhudeb and Ramgati Nyayratna. Then in 1868, Bhudeb found himself the editor of the *Education Gazette*, which had been started in July 1856 as a government organ with support from the then Inspector of Schools, Hodgson Pratt. Though Bhudeb had been Pratt's first choice as founding editor, the Education Department passed him over and handed the editorship successively to the Rev. O'Brien Smith and then Pyaricharan Sarkar. When Pyaricharan demitted office over an article criticising the government's response to a railway accident, Bhudeb was requested to take up the baton. However, Bhudeb was prepared to do so only on his own terms. As a result, the government agreed to turn over all rights and assets of the press to Bhudeb, along with a one-time subvention of 300 rupees.[91] Following this, Bhudeb brought the periodical to Hooghly and started printing it from his press. This too was only the second instance of a periodical originally started in Calcutta being relocated to a district press (the first was the famous *Somprakash*).

Fortunately, we have some idea about the print runs of the *Gazette*. A report by Hodgson Pratt of January 1857 notes that the *Gazette* had a circulation of 370 in the mofussil and 107 in Calcutta bringing the total print run to 477.[92] When official print runs become available from August 1877, we find the *Gazette* logging exactly 1,168 copies. The figure dipped to 800 sometime in the 1880s but again rose to 1,350 by the end of the century, making the *Gazette* the only provincial periodical to have a circulation in four figures. The *Gazette* also turned out to be one of the longest running periodicals of its time, with Bhudeb's descendants issuing it into the fourth decade of the twentieth century.

The *Education Gazette* was not the first periodical to be printed from Hooghly-Chinsurah though. In January 1858, the *Gazette* (still being printed from Calcutta) reported on the launch of a fortnightly from

---

[90] *Bhudeb Charit*, 197–8.   [91] Kumar, *Bangsha parichay*, vol. 1, 101–2.
[92] 'Appendix A', *General Report on Public Instruction*, 58.

Chinsurah titled *Subodhini*, priced at four annas and edited by Ramchandra Dicchit. Later, Akshaychandra Sarkar, editor of the famous *Sadharani*, would recall the editor as a 'Hindustani brahman' who was fluent in Sanskrit and Bengali. The paper was written in lucid Bengali, and was printed in two columns in foolscap size.[93] After a couple of years, Dicchit handed over the editorship to a local pundit of Sanskrit whose bombastic Bengali led to a rapid fall of circulation and consequent demise of the periodical.

But it was Naihati across the river that was the site of two of the most well-known periodicals in the district. The first was the *Bangadarshan*, founded by Bankimchandra Chatterjee, father of the modern Bengali novel, in 1872. Bankimchandra, then at the height of his literary powers, had arrived in Berhampore in 1870 as deputy magistrate. There he gathered a glittering literary constellation around himself, comprising the likes of Ramdas Sen, Loharam Shiroratna, Rajrkrishna Mukhopdahyay, Dinabandhu Mitra and a young Akshaychandra Sarkar, among others.[94] The arrival of *Bangadarshan* in April 1872 was a landmark in Bengali letters. At first, it was printed from the Saptahik Sangbad press in Bhawanipur, Calcutta, but soon Sanjibchandra, the novelist's younger brother, established a printing press at their family house in Kanthalpara, Naihati. Naming the press Bangadarshan turned out to be a self-fulfilling prophecy, as Bankimchandra was persuaded to shift the printing of *Bangadarshan* to the family press in from April 1873. At this time, each monthly issue of the periodical ran to forty-eight pages in royal octavo, and was priced at eight annas. The print run was 1,500. In April the following year, the press added another periodical to its list, the *Bhramar*, edited by Sanjibchandra. At its zenith, Bangadarshan's reach and reputation was unparalleled. Sandip Datta finds a list of 145 subscribers in the issue of February 1873, in both Calcutta as well as mofussil locations such as Kumilla, Barishal, Dacca, Mymensingh, Burdwan, Birbhum, Narail, Khagra, Sirajgunj, Baharampur, Barasat, Pabna, Chattagram, Bankipur, Tamluk, Memari, Natore, Kamarpur, Muradpur and Tirhoot. Outside Bengal, there were subscribers in

[93] Brajendranath, *BSP 1801–68*, 154.

[94] Bagal, 'Bankimchandra chattopadhyay', 16.

Kanpur, Lucknow, Allahabad, Tripura, Mokama, Munger, Baleshwar, Varanasi and so on.[95]

Despite the tremendous prestige and influence of *Bangadarshan*, the Bangadarshan Press was not exactly a model of fiscal discipline. After four years under the editorship of Bankimchandra, the magazine suspended publication for a while, in March 1876; when it resumed, the editorship was taken over by brother Sanjibchandra. However, the second innings of the magazine was marked by erratic appearances, and Bankimchandra minced no words in laying the blame at his brother's door. It was not in Sanjibchandra's nature to stick at one thing, and his inattention towards the press meant that some of the press employees – 'who should have been kept under supervision' – had free rein, playing havoc with the income of the press.[96] Eventually, both *Bangadarshan* and the press perished – a peculiar instance of a press that failed to last despite having so much going for it.

The second press in the region, also of a humanist persuasion, was Akshaychandra Sarkar's *Sadharani*. Akshaychandra, a law graduate from Calcutta, went to Berhampore after his graduation in 1868 to join his father's legal practice. But the world of letters seemed to hold more attraction for the young Akshaychandra, who immediately became part of Bankimchandra's literary circle, and contributed an article in the very first issue of *Bangadarshan* in 1872. Later that year, Akshaychandra returned to Chinsurah upon his mother's illness and opted not to return to Berhampore. The following year, in November 1873, he decided to follow in Bankim's footsteps by founding a weekly titled *Sadharani*. At first, the periodical was printed from the Bangadarshan Press but in July 1874, Akshaychandra acquired a printing press of his own and housed it in a rented house adjacent to his own. In the next issue (July 1874), he wrote ecstatically, though somewhat incoherently: 'This issue of *Sadharani* is printed from the new Sadharani Press. No reader can imagine our state of mind; we will not reveal our state of mind to those who cannot imagine it.'[97]

---

[95] Datta, *Bangla samayikpatrer itibritta*, 37–8.

[96] Bankimchandra, *Sanjibani sudha*, quoted in 'Sanjibchandra Chattopadhyay', *SSC* vol. 3, 32.

[97] Quoted in Brajendranath, 'Akshaychandra Sarkar', *SSC* vol. 3, 26.

Along with printing the weekly, Akshaychandra made good use of the press. Somewhat predictably, the first two books issued by the press were by the Sarkar son and father respectively. Akshaychandra's offering (August 1874) was a book of translated verses – mostly of Byron – carried out in his student days. The following year, *Ritubarnan*, a book of verses by Gangacharan Sarkar was issued by the press. This is a curious production, with the title-page announcing that the first fifty-odd pages were printed from the Johnson's Press in Calcutta, and the remaining at Sadharani. This is followed by no less than four errata pages, with all the errors belonging in the first half of the book. No doubt filial piety had prompted Akshaychandra to rescue his father's book from the typographical hell into which it had fallen, but the sheets had already been printed, and could not be completely discarded. But it is from the pages of *Sadharani* that we get a sense of an incipient community of letters. The issue of 23 August 1874, for example, advertised the wares of the Bangadarshan Press, and an upcoming periodical titled *Hindubilashi*. The 'News' column featured detailed despatches from local correspondents of remote mofussil locations. In contrast, national and international news were compressed to one-sentence paragraphs appearing in random sequence; thus, the news of an earthquake in Yokohama is succeeded by the news that all of the poet Michael Madhusudan Dutt's copyrights had been auctioned at the Town Hall and sold to Benimadhab De & Co. for 3,300 rupees.[98]

For a decade from its founding, there was hardly an idle hour at the Sadharani Press. In particular, it seemed to have been the go-to press for a number of quality periodicals: the *Prachin kabyasamgraha*, a monthly compendium of ancient poetry (1874); *Binodini*, a monthly miscellany (1875); the Rev. Lal Behari Dey's *Bengal Magazine* (1875); the one issue of the satirical *Panchananda* that 'blazed like a meteor' before disappearing (1878); and the *Bengal Miscellany* (1882). Other presses in Chinsurah took to the periodical form with enthusiasm: the *Chikitsa darpan* (1871) printed by the Chikitsa Prakash Press, a press specialising in medical publishing; the monthly *Chinshura prakashika* (1871); the monthly *Ajijan nehar* (1874), edited by the remarkable Mir Mosharraf Hossain with a group of 'Muslim

---

[98] 'Sangbad', *Sadharani*, 4 October 1874, 298.

youth from the Hooghly College';[99] the monthly *Hindubilasi* (1874); and the *Kumudini* (1874). It seemed that Hooghly, which had belatedly caught up with printing, was making up for lost time with a vengeance.

In July 1884, a malaria-weakened Akshaychandra decided to move the press to Calcutta. With the moving-out of the Sadharani Press from Chinsurah, an era in mofussil printing came to an end.

~

Life after the Baptists: Serampore Redux

Though the Mission Press waned in the 1830s, printing continued to flourish in Serampore without a break. In January 1826, the missionary-run *Samachar darpan* reported that a certain Nilmani Halder of Chinsurah had set up a printing press in Serampore;[100] after Gangakishore's Bangal Gejeti Press's relocation to Bahara, this is likely the first instance of a press set up by indigenous initiative outside Calcutta. The first book to be printed from the press was a compilation by Nilmani's son Nilratan in 1826, ambitiously titled 'Bohoordurson, or Various Spectacles, Being A choice collection of Proverbs and Morals in the English, Latin, Bengalee, Sanscrit, Persian and Arabic *languages*'. The Bengali printing press was often the site of filial or parental indulgence, though Nilmani did earn his own spurs by going on to edit the periodical *Bangadut* (est. 1829), and authoring nearly a dozen books.

In June 1854, the newspaper *Sambad bhaskar*, in an adulatory article on Nilratna Halder, observed that his father Nilmani had been a 'famous man of wealth'.[101] Nilmani's brother Prankrishna too had been one of the wealthiest men in Chinsurah and was noted for his philanthropy.[102] It is therefore unlikely that Nilmani set up the press with the aim of making money, but more as a launch-pad for his son's literary career. Perhaps owing to the lack a profit motive, we do not see much activity in the press

[99] Brajendranath, *BSP 1818–68*, 14. [100] Brajendranath, *SSK* vol. 1, 37.

[101] Brajendranath, 'Nilratna Haldar', *SSC* vol. 1, 487.

[102] Mitra, *Hooghly jelar itihas*, 602. The Halder brothers also served jail terms for forging promissory notes.

after 1830, and Serampore had to wait another nine years before the coming of a press that would become perhaps the most storied among all district presses. This was founded by the legendary Karmakar family, which had for three generations cut type for the Serampore Baptists.

In 1842, the *Asiatic Journal and Monthly Miscellany*, citing a report from the *Friend of India*, published the following under the headline 'Native Ingenuity':

> A native of Calcutta, by hereditary profession a blacksmith, who was employed for many years in cutting punches for this press . . . has manufactured an iron press . . . and set up a printing-office, at which he has commenced printing for the country at large. Last year, he printed a native almanac of a superior character, which had a remarkable run. Soon after this he began to engrave on lead pictures of the gods and goddesses of the Hindoo Pantheon, of which hundreds of thousands were struck off on inferior paper, and obtained a ready sale. . . . Hawkers were employed in traversing the country with packs of these mythological prints . . . The supply, however, soon became too great for the demand, and his competitors relinquished the trade, which has since languished, and is now confined to a very limited extent. But his ingenuity was not extinguished. He determined to print English books for the numerous youths of the poorer classes, who are now endeavouring to obtain a smattering of our own tongue, and from whom even the low-priced elementary works of the Calcutta School-Book Society are too high. Of these works, thousands of pirated copies have been printed in Calcutta, and disseminated throughout the country. But the individual we allude to, finding English type at second-hand too dear at his purpose, has cut a set of punches for himself, and cast the types which he employs for his work.[103]

---

[103] 'Native Ingenuity', 27.

The blacksmith referred to in the report was Krishnachandra Karmakar and the press in question was the Chandroday Press, founded in 1839 by the Karmakar family. As the report indicates, Krishnachandra had several irons in the fire. There is reference to 'an almanac of superior character'. As Gautam Bhadra has pointed out, the Chandroday Press was the most important player in the almanacs market, issuing them from as early as 1840, with Krishnachandra himself designing and engraving the images.[104] The Rev. Long refers to a 'Serampore almanac, began 1840',[105] which ran to 234 pages and was priced at four annas. Long estimated that 4,000 copies of the almanac had been sold till the mid-1850s, and as far afield as Assam, Benaras and Rungpore.

Krishnachandra's engravings for his almanacs – especially of the goddess Durga and Hindu festivals – established a visual protocol that would prove to be remarkably long-lasting. Chittaranjan Bandyopadhyay argues that the image of the goddess Durga in the 1842 Chandroday Press almanac continued to be reproduced in modern-day almanacs and is the forerunner of the iconography of the community *pujas* of the goddess to this day.[106] Then there is reference to the new market of printed mythological prints that Krishnachandra appears to have founded. Finally, there are the cheap text-books with which Krishnachandra allegedly tried to undercut the market of the CSBS. The last-named is likely a reference to an 1841 edition of *Niti-katha* or moral tales originally published from the CSBS in 1818. It was also very likely pirated. In one of its annual reports, the CSBS noted ruefully that '(n)ative booksellers . . . used to pirate some of its most useful and popular works, and print them with the Society's imprimatur C.S.B. S. upon the title-page'.[107] The distinctive CSBS colophon was possibly the first in Bengali printing, and was often imitated or copied.

The untimely death of Krishnachandra in the 1840s was a blow to the Chandroday Press and it never regained its primacy in terms of almanacs

---

[104] Bhadra, 'Celestial and Worldly Time', 291. See also Bhadra, *Nyara battlaay jay kobar?*, 419.

[105] Long, *Descriptive Catalogue*, 62.

[106] Bhadra, 'Pictures in Celestial and Worldly Time', 206.

[107] *Seventeenth Report*, 15.

publishing, with Calcutta printers such as Nrityalal Sil and Benimadhab Dey moving to take its place. However, the Karmakar family maintained its excellence in typecasting and Krishnachandra's brothers Ramchandra and Harachandra set up the Adhar Type Foundry which was a going concern till the end of the twentieth century. From 1852, the press also got going in the periodicals market, issuing the monthly *Gyanarunoday* from January 1852. The editors were two Serampore notables, Kalidas Moitra and Jadunath Chattopadhyay. The former demitted his charge after a year in office and the periodical closed for a while. The new series began in April 1854 under Jadunath's editorship. The second periodical to be issued by the press – just four months after the first, in July 1852 – was the *Sambad sasadhar*, which purported to be a digest of news and views published in the world press, rendered into simple Bengali. The annual subscription was a somewhat steep six rupees and it was no surprise that the periodical did not last for more than a year, leading the *Samvad pravakar* to comment unkindly that the *Sasadhar* (lit. the moon) had been 'eclipsed by clouds'.[108]

After the Chandroday Press, the baton of Serampore printing passed into the hands of the Tamohar Press, and its printer J. H. Peters (succeeded by B. M. Sen in the late 1860s). Little is known about the origins and ownership of the press, though its name (lit. dispeller of darkness) suggests that it might have had missionary origins. From the 1850s, the 'Tomohur' Press (as it was called) printed in a wide variety of subjects – plays, poetry, pedagogy, course books, law reports and the like. To a modern observer two titles stand out – both pamphlets opposing Ishwarchandra Bidyasagar's campaign to legalise the remarriage of Hindu widows (which became law in 1855).[109] Why a Serampore press would lend its efforts to the conservative rump of Hindu society is not clear, unless it was to do with the figure of Kalidas Moitra – one of the pamphleteers – who published at least half a dozen titles with the press between 1855 and 1862. Notable among these were three titles under the so-called 'Day's Courses', a set of textbooks funded by brothers Harishchandra and Srinath Dey on subjects such as 'The

[108] Brajendranath, *BSP 1818–68*, 125–8.

[109] These were the *Bidhababibahabad* (1854) and the *Pounarbhaba khandanam* (1855) by Kalidas Maitra.

Electric Telegraph' (1855), 'The Steam Engine and the East India Railway' (1855) and 'Geography' (1857). Both brothers were scions of the renowned Dey family in Serampore, noted for their philanthropy as well as their adherence to traditional Hindu practice. The family founded two presses in Serampore, one of which printed the *Indian Reformer* magazine, edited by the folklorist and novelist Rev. Lalbehari Dey, and set up in 1861 to attack Brahomism, a monotheistic sect led by Keshab Chandra Sen.[110] The other press reportedly printed the monthly *Bigyanmihiroday*[111] (est. April 1857), edited by another Serampore notable Narayan Chattaraj Gunanidhi.[112] Chattaraj, like Moitra, frequently acknowledged the patronage of the Dey brothers in the title-pages of his books, variously issued from Serampore and Burdwan.

The textbooks for the 'Day's Courses' failed to find their desired market, however. These were reportedly submitted to the government for inclusion in the curriculum, but the list was referred to Bidyasagar who considered them unsuitable for classroom use. It has been speculated that Maitra's opposition to widow remarriage may have been a factor behind Bidyasagar's decision.[113] In any case, Maitra was likely acting at the behest of the Dey family, whose conservative Hinduism would necessarily put them at odds with Bidyasgar's reformism as well as the Brahmo movement. At the same time, the Deys were also lending their names to textbooks on modern technologies such as the railway and telegraphy, donating liberally to both English and vernacular schools, and supporting scholarships at the local missionary-run collegiate school. The Dey family's model of patronage was not uncommon in nineteenth-century Bengal, but what is noteworthy was their direct involvement in publishing, and the active mobilisation of print in the service of their agenda. In their attempt, albeit

---

[110] Sen Gupta, *Folklorists of Bengal*, 19.

[111] According to Brajendranath, the periodical was printed from the Tamohar Press; see *BSP 1818–68*, 151–2.

[112] *Bangsha-parichay*, vol. 2, 256.

[113] Comment by 'Elebele', in 'Elebele' (pseud.) *Dwishotoborshe bidyasagar*, ch. 10, *Guruchandali*. www.guruchandali.com/comment.php?topic=19780. Accessed 12 March 2021.

failed, to break into textbooks, do we also see the mounting of challenge from the mofussil directed at the city's stranglehold over the lucrative textbooks market?

In time, the Deys would also come to own another printing establishment, the Alfred Press, established in 1870 by the geographer Sashibhushan Chattopadhyay from neighbouring Konnagar. Though the first few titles reflected the expertise of the proprietor, the press soon changed hands, successively to Jadunath Banerjee, and finally to Harishchandra Dey, whose name then appears frequently in the *Bengal Library Catalogue* as the copyright assignee of most of the press's imprints. In 1871, the press began printing the fortnightly *Halisahar patrika*, a reputed periodical issued from a town about fifty miles north of Calcutta, as well as the occasional issue of the *Chikitsa darpan*, a medical journal In 1873, it launched a monthly devoted to Vedic and Puranic commentary titled *Sarbbarthasambgraha* but its most ambitious project was the serial publication of the *Mahabharata*, translated by Sridhar Churamani, and published in forty-page fascicles (eight annas, Royal octavo, usually 700 copies). Till August 1888, it had published 128 instalments of the epic and had reached the 'Dronaparba'.[114] Unlike the other Mahabharata projects of its time (see 'Burdwan' below), these fascicles were not distributed gratis but circulated by way of trade.

~

Patronage and Print: Burdwan

The case of Burdwan presents an anomaly as far as printing in the districts is concerned. Despite being an early starter in setting up presses, printing in Burdwan largely remained a province of the royal family, for at least half a century. The *Burdwan District Gazetteer* of 1910 noted that there were only 'four public printing presses in Burdwan, two at Asansol, and two at Raniganj'.[115] This might be one instance where the success of courtly printing overshadowed the growth of indigenous initiative.

---

[114] *Bengal Library Catalogue of Books for the Third Quarter Ending 30th September 1888*, 70.

[115] Peterson, *District Gazetteers: Burdwan*, 182.

Printing in Burdwan began in earnest during the occupancy of Mahatab Chand Bahadur, adopted son of the previous incumbent Tej Chand Bahadur, who died in 1832. The Burdwan Raj had been founded by Sangam Rai Kapoor, a Khatri from Kotli in Punjab, in 1657. In 1760, the zamindari of Burdwan was ceded to the East India Company after a failed uprising, and subsequently, its relation with the Company was one of mutual accommodation and benefit. The house prospered after the Permanent Settlement, particularly after the giving away of portions of the zamindari on perpetual lease, or *patnis*.[116] The first book to be published under the auspices of the Burdwan Raj was in 1830, towards the end of Tej Chandra Bahadur's occupancy. This was the lavishly illustrated *Hariharmangal samgit*, compiled by Paranchand Kapoor, the *dewan* of the royal family, featuring seventy-two engravings by Ramdhan Swarnakar of Calcutta, the leading engraver of the day.[117]

It was to be nearly two decades before printing returned to Burdwan, in the form of a clutch of periodicals in 1849–50. A bi-weekly, the *Sambad bardhaman gyanpradiyni* (ed. Bisheswar Mukhopadhyay), and the weekly *Bardhaman Chandroday* (ed. Ramtaran Bhattcharya) both debuted in December 1849.[118] It is not clear though whether these were printed in Burdwan. But there is no such doubt about the weekly *Sambad bardhaman* which began publication from September 1850, on a press of the same name, and with funding from the palace. Its arrival was noted with pleasure by the aforementioned *Gyanpradayini*, which commended the editor (Kalidas Bandyopadhyay) for printing the periodical on a new press, with new type and woodcuts, and for sparing no expense.[119] According to Long, the yearly subscription of the periodical was four rupees.[120]

Not much else is known about the first press in Burdwan, the Sambad Bardhaman Press, other than one curious production. In 1858, a zamindar from nearby Baidyapur, Dinabandhu Nandy Majumdar, commissioned a forgettable work on Hindu mythology titled *Sarbbacittaranjan*, written

---

[116] Ibid., 48–9. [117] Sarkar, 'Bardhaman raj o bardhamaner prakashana'.
[118] Brajendranath, *BSP 1818–68*, 108. [119] Ibid., 117–8.
[120] Long, *Descriptive Catalogue*, 69.

by one Chandrakumar Chakrabarty.[121] The title-page mentioned that the book might be had from the *kutcheri* house of the 'said honourable' baboo,[122] a common practice with early Bengali title-pages. The book was unpriced, from which it is fairly certain that it was given away free by the zamindar as an act of piety, as well as aspiration. Swapan Chakravorty has pointed out how such gratis distribution of books recall the practice of giving away *puthis* or manuscript books during the pre-print period. But while such *puthis* would traditionally gifted to a 'select caste', the advent of print saw copies being given away 'irrespective of caste'.[123] Such was the case when Kaliprasanna Singha, one of the brightest lights of the 'Bengal renaissance', financed the publication and free distribution of seventeen volumes of the Sanskrit epic *Mahabharata* during 1860–66. Matching Kaliprasanna was Mahtab Chand, the Maharaja of Burdwan with his free distribution of 'Sanskrit, Persian and Urdu books'.[124]

Mahtab Chand's foray into the world of publishing began in 1854, with the printing of the 'Adikanda' of the Sanskrit epic *Ramayana*. The Sambad Bardhaman Press was not deemed suitable for this purpose, and the contract went to the Bhaskar Press of Calcutta, which printed at least two *khandas* of the epic in 1854 and 1857. But the court soon acquired several state-of-the-art printing presses and began the task of issuing both the epics, under the editorship of a group of court pundits. The *Mahabharata* was issued between 1862 and 1873 in twenty-two parts and eight volumes, after some of the early volumes were scrapped in the interests of quality control.[125] The volumes were printed in folio with print runs varying between 500 to 1,500, and the total number of pages running to a staggering 2,299 pages.[126]

---

[121] 'The publication does no credit to the Burdwan Press, as every page of the book is filled with typographical mistakes', wrote the *Calcutta Review*, vol. 32 (1859), xvii.

[122] The family and the house are both extant.

[123] Chakravorty, 'Purity and Print', 206–7. [124] Ibid.

[125] See 'Old Indian Arts' at www.oldindianarts.in/2011/10/illustrations-from-barddhaman-edition.html for woodcuts from the Burdwan Mahabharata.

[126] Blumhardt, *Catalogue of Bengali Printed Books*, 60.

The printing at the Burdwan court was divided among a number of presses. The epics were assigned to the Satyaprakash Press and its printer Purusottam Deb Chattaraj. Another court press, the Adhiraj, was also under his charge. The Khasjantra (printer Umeshchandra Chattopadhyay) accounted for translations of Persian tales such as *Hatem tai* (published 1861). According to Sukumar Sen, the Khasjantra was used chiefly in printing forms and stationery. The other reputable press in Burdwan was the Aryama Press.[127] This seems to have been the one press in Burdwan that was outside the ambit of the court, as all of its publications were priced. For example, its first title *Chittabinod*[128] was published in 1869 in an edition of 1,000 and priced at ten annas, while its second title *Jagat kanda* published in the same year had a print run of 500 and cost four annas. In September 1866, it was also responsible for printing the *Bardhaman masik patrika*, a monthly organ of the Brahmo Samaj of Burdwan. But it ceased publication towards the end of 1867, and merged with *Shiksha darpan*, edited by Bhudeb Mukhopadhyay.[129]

The Satyaprakash Press and its printer Puruoshottam Deb Chattaraj were active till 1889 but there seemed to be little printing – at least of books – in Burdwan in the last decade of the nineteenth century. In any case, the Satyaprakash Press did not do any job-work in its catchment area, as all of its imprints were unpriced, as indicated by the entries in the quarterly *Bengali Library* catalogue issued from 1867. After Aryama Press, the only press that printed commercially in Burdwan was the Bardhaman Press (prop. Pyarilal Sinha),[130] which printed the occasional periodical as well, such as the short-lived *Pracharika* in 1870 (average print run: 165), and the more successful *Bardhaman sanjivani* from 1878. The latter in particular was noted for its persistent criticism of government policies, and was one of the very few district newspapers to last till the

---

[127] Sen, 'Battalar boi', 275.

[128] The author of the work was one Ishan Chandra Basu, who was also the printer. This was not the only example of printers/proprietors issuing their own works through the press.

[129] Brajendranath, *BSP 1818–68*, 209–10. [130] 'Literature and the Press', cciv.

end of the century. For most of its life, its circulation stood at 300 before slightly dipping to about 250 in 1899.

According to the *Bengal Library Catalogue*, a sum total of only five books were printed from Burdwan presses in the entire decade of 1890–99: most books that were published from Burdwan were printed from Calcutta. Even the productions of the Burdwan court, such as the varied oeuvre of Bijay Chand Mahatab, were published from Calcutta presses.

~

Changaripota: A Railway Story

In the general history of printing in the mofussil, it is tempting to speculate that the phenomenon took off following the establishment of a railway network over much of southern Bengal from the mid-1850s. The dates of the presses would seem to suggest so, but we also have to remember that in many cases the river[131] – or even the bullock-cart – was an easier mode of transport for print machinery. However, in at least one case, the coming of the railways was directly responsible for the relocation of a press from Calcutta to a rural wilderness. This was the press set up by Dwarakanath Vidyabhushan for the printing of *Somprakash*, one of the most influential periodicals of the day.

Dwarakanath (b. 1819) came from the village of Changaripota, about a dozen miles south of Calcutta, in the present-day South 24-Parganas. After studying in Calcutta's Sanskrit College, he quickly rose to the post of a second professorship at the same college, and became an assistant to Ishwarchandra Bidyasagar. It was at Bidyasagar's suggestion that Dwarkanath founded the weekly *Somprakash*, the most influential periodical of its time, in November 1858. Initially, it was printed from a press in Chanpatala, Calcutta, which had been set up in 1856 by Dwarkanath's father, Harachandra. In 1862, a new railway line from the city's Sealdah station to Port Canning – the Matla railway – brought Changaripota within commuting distance (the nearest railway station was Sonarpur).

---

[131] Ashis Khastagir reports on how it took a month for a printing press to travel by water from Calcutta to Mymensingh in 1875. *Bangla chapakhana*, 41.

Dwarkanath forthwith brought the press home to his village and started issuing *Somprakash* from there every Monday. In her account of the Indian press, Uma Das Gupta describes how such newspapers such as the *Somprakash* were run more or less with a skeleton staff by the proprietor-editor: 'Dwarkanath ... spent his days in the Sanskrit College in Calcutta, where he taught, while the nights were reserved for writing articles for the journal. He had a sub-editor, who compiled the week's news and received the letters and saw the papers through the press every Sunday. But Vidyabhushan alone wrote all the articles.'[132]

A lively account of the setting-up of the press can be found in *Atmacharit*,[133] the autobiography of Dwarkanath's nephew Sibnath Sastri. Sastri also mentions how his first experience of journalism was to edit *Somprakash* for nearly a year when his uncle was away in Benaras in 1873. Sastri took this opportunity to agitate for municipal reforms in the columns of *Somprakash*. Despite being notionally part of a municipality, Changaripota and its adjacent villages were a malarious wilderness and did not even have a single paved road between themselves.[134] Thanks to Sastri's campaign, the Rajpur municipality was set up in 1873, and when the south-eastern railways was extended to Diamond Harbour, the village got a railway station of its own (modern-day Subhasgram).[135]

Till the coming of *Somprakash*, the world of Bengali periodicals had a distinctly Augustan flavour about it, with scurrility and no-holds-barred name-calling the norm. Almost overnight, *Somprakash* set a new bar for a serious and engaged public discourse. It moved effortlessly between the local, national and the international issues, in a language and tone that signalled a complete break from the preceding. At the same time, it was a relentless commentator on political questions. Bipin Chandra Pal, the Indian nationalist, wrote: 'Government servants were not as yet strictly forbidden to have any manner of connection with the newspaper press. ... *Somprakas* [sic] was ... a professedly political newspaper, and it had always been absolutely outspoken in its criticism of public policies and

---

[132] Das Gupta, 'The Indian Press 1870–1880', 217. [133] Sastri, *Atmacharit*, 63.
[134] Ibid., 170–1. [135] Brajendranath, 'Dwarkanath Bidyabhushan', *SSC* vol. 1, 251.

measures.'[136] It is not surprising, therefore, that one of the first casualties of the Vernacular Press Act of 1878 was the *Somprakash*. Under the provisions of this act, introduced for the 'better control of publications in Oriental languages' and passed during the incumbency of Lord Lytton, a number of newspaper and periodicals were asked to provide bail-bonds. Significantly, many of these were mofussil papers, such as the *Somprakash*, the *Sadharani* of Chinsurah, and the *Bharat mihir* of Mymensingh. In its issue of 24 March 1879, the *Somprakash* wrote:

> It is difficult to continue its publication with a sword drawn
> over its head . . . The rulers have now become fault-finding;
> they do not judge any writing by its spirit. . . . we [had]
> determined to stop the publication of this paper; but on the
> advice of friends, and inasmuch as no communication has
> directly been addressed to us, we have given up the idea, and
> resolved not to cease from our labour until we have been
> fully informed of the offence for which a bond and a deposit
> have been asked of us.[137]

For the next few weeks, the Bengali-language press was in ferment over the imminent demise of the *Somprakash*, and the newspaper was closed down in April 1879. Along with it passed the year-old *Dibakar* from Birbhum, which was closed for supporting *Somprakash* in its columns. *Bharat mihir*, a fellow-traveller, lamented: 'The *Somprakash* is no more, and the right-hand of the vernacular press has been cut off. That Lord Lytton, the son of the author of *Rienzi*, himself a poet, should thus have destroyed with his own hand an important member of the newspaper press of a country, is verily a sad thought.'[138] It would be another year before the *Somprakash* would reappear, in April 1880. But it was no longer as influential as it was, and soon changed ownership.[139]

Another feature of *Somprakash* that is particularly relevant to this study is that it published the names and locations of its subscribers. The periodical

[136] Pal, *Memories of my Life and Times*, 306. [137] RNP, No. 13 of 1879, 11.
[138] RNP, No. 16 of 1879, 7. [139] Sastri, *Ramtanu Lahiri*, 192.

specified that it would only deliver copies in the 'mofussil' to those who would pay an advance subscription, to the tune of ten rupees annually, or five rupees biannually, the latter being the minimum subscription. Every weekly issue would carry the names and address of new subscribers on its last page, giving us a clear idea about readers in the mofussil. For instance, in the issue of 17 November 1862, the following names may be seen to appear: Krishnanath Saha of Kumarkhali, Kilby Saintsbury of Jessore, Dwarkanath Ray of Jessore, Sheetalchandra Sett of Sibpur and Durgacharan Nandy of China Bazaar. Thus, from the available issues of *Somparakash*, it should be possible to recover the subscription base of the periodical in the provinces.

Despite blazing such a trail, the *Somprakash* was not the first periodical to be published from the South 24-Parganas. In 1856, a group of young men led by one Haripada Datta had started a periodical called the *Majilpur patrika* from the village of the same name. Sibnath Sastri, who was then a boy of nine, recalls that the periodical 'ran for a while'.[140] Four years later in 1860, nearby Rajpur too launched a short-lived monthly titled *Rajpur patrika*.

~

The Village Rises: Kumarkhali

The case of Kumarkhali's *Grambarta prakashika* (est. April 1863) and its heroic editor 'Kangal' Harinath Majumdar is probably the most storied in the annals of newspapers in Bengal. The *Grambarta* was the first newspaper with a stated aim of representing the interests of the peasantry and the rural populace at large. Brajendranath Bandypoadhyay quotes from the unpublished – and now presumed lost – journal of Harinath where the latter refers to a government decision to translate the contents of Bengali newspapers, and create the post of a Bengali translator for the purpose: 'It was my intention to start a newspaper to ventilate the grievances of the rural populace to the ears of the government, whereupon they would no doubt address such issues and strive for the common weal of the people.'[141]

Harinath was no stranger to journalism. His day job was that of a poorly paid schoolmaster, but he regularly despatched copy to two of Calcutta's

---

[140] Ibid., 25. [141] Brajendranath, *BSP 1818–68*, 181.

leading newspapers – the *Hindoo Patriot* of Harish Mukherjee and the *Samvad pravakar* of Ishwarchandra Gupta. Akshaykumar Maitreya, a later editor of *Grambarta*, writes how his father, Mathuranath, and Harinath sent regular reports from the mofussil during the indigo rebellion.[142] Another future editor and Akshaykumar's childhood friend, Jaladhar Sen, was to write:

> At that time, neither Harinath or anyone in the mofussil possessed a printing press. There was no easy way to travel to Calcutta, nor had the railways started operations in eastern Bengal. At such a time, it took tremendous courage to publish a newspaper which would be printed in Calcutta. The general people did not read newspapers much, in fact most of them did not even know what newspapers were for. Owing to the high price of newspapers, no one save the rich had the means to acquire them.[143]

In the beginning, the *Grambarta* was a monthly newspaper and was printed from the Girish Bidyaratna Press in Calcutta, but it successively turned fortnightly in 1869 and weekly in 1879. For much of its life, the newspaper struggled to keep itself afloat, chiefly owing to difficulties in collecting subscriptions. Harinath, who was a poorly paid village school-teacher, frequently went into debt to keep the newspaper running. Nevertheless, he was able to set up a printing press in Kumarkhali in 1873, called the Mathuranath Press. It soldiered on for six years before Harinath closed down the weekly edition in May 1879, only retaining the monthly edition. In an editorial of April 1880, Harinath referred to a host of reasons for the closure, such as the 'distant thunder of press regulations on the firmament of India' (this referred to the Vernacular Press Act of 1878), 'the general apathy towards Bengali newspapers' and 'unwillingness to pay subscriptions on time' – all of which had prostrated the editor with worry and disease.[144]

---

[142] Maitreya, 'Akshaykumar Maitreyar banghsa pairchay', in Basu, *Banger jatiya itihas: burendra brahman-bibaran*, 183.

[143] Sen, *Kangal harinath*, 10. [144] Quoted in Brajendranath, *BSP 1818–68*, 183.

However, *Grambarta* would not go so easily, and thanks to the efforts of a number of local allies, the weekly was revived from April 1882. This time the editors were two young men from the village who had already begun to make their mark in the world of letters, Jaladhar Sen and Akshaykumar Maitryea. It carried on for another three years before finally ceasing publication in the autumn of 1885. Like most other mofussil periodicals, the print run of the *Grambarta* hovered around the 200 mark till the early 1880s, though there was a surge to 500 in 1885 before folding up in the same year.

One of the reasons behind the *Grambarta*'s precariousness was its relentless criticism of the landed interest and the police. Kumarkhali was located close to the zamindari estate of Debendranath Tagore, a leading light of the Brahmo Samaj and father of Rabindranath Tagore. Harinath clashed frequently with the Tagore estate, as he refused to moderate his criticism of Debendranath for oppressing his tenantry. In December 1878, for instance, the following was noted by the Bengali Translator's Office:

> A recent case has occurred in the *Zamindari* of *Babu Debendranath Tagore*, in *Birahimpore Pargunnah*, where the complaints of certain oppressed tenants have been referred to the *zamindari amlahs* for enquiry. These men hissing like snakes that have been trodden on, threaten to avenge themselves on the petitioners. The *mafussal* peasant is treated like a fish; no mercy is shown him the moment he is seen.[145]

Elsewhere we have written that the *Grambarta* 'devoted itself almost exclusively to rural issues, highlighting atrocities against the peasants by planters, zamindars and the administration. It was particularly critical of city-based periodicals that increasingly represented the interests of the landed gentry, such as the *Hindoo Patriot* and even the redoubtable *Amritabazar Patrika*'.[146] This conscious positioning of *Grambarta* against

[145] RNP, No. 52 of 1878, 8.
[146] Ray and Gupta, 'The Newspaper and the Periodical Press in Colonial India', 259.

the vested interests of the landholding class and city newspapers is a landmark moment in the history of print journalism in India.

Another notable feature of *Grambarta*'s journalism was its willingness to travel afield in search of copy. In his journal, Harinath mentions that instead of relying on word of mouth, he would often travel – sometimes incognito – to locations like Santipur, Chakda, Mehrepur and Ula to report on local histories, as well as the spread of epidemic.[147] *Grambarta* also encouraged local correspondents, notably Mir Mosharraf Hossain, one of the leaders among a new generation of progressive writers who made common cause with the oppressed peasantry. Mosharraf, who was born in Kushtia in 1847, cut his journalistic teeth as a local correspondent for both the *Grambarta* as well as the *Sambad prabhakar* of Calcutta in the mid-1860s. In his autobiography, Mosharraf wrote:

> I lived close to Kumarkhali. Harinath Majumdar, the editor, was like an elder brother to me. ... I wrote for the *Grambarta* every week, as well as for the *Prabhakar*. I was then in Moktarpur (in Jessore) with not much to do. I would go around collecting news and filing despatches. Harinath-babu wrote to me, asking me to file a story on the Kapotaksha river ... I would go long distances by boat and write. He would then edit the copy and publish in his newspaper.[148]

In April 1874, Mir Mosharraf Hossain and a few students from Hooghly College started a periodical called *Ajijan nehar* in Chinsurah. It was arguably the first Bengali periodical to be founded by a Muslim. In his unpublished autobiography, Mosharraf described how a chance encounter with Bankimchandra Chattopadhyay near the Chinsurah ferry led to its publication; the writer had deplored the lack of a periodical which voiced Muslim opinion. Harinath, who had been encouraging of Mosharraf throughout, reported on the new periodical in the *Grambarta* of April 1874. Most other

[147] Brajendranath, *BSP 1818–68*, 183.

[148] Quoted in 'Mir Mosharraf Hossain', *SSC 2*, 443.

journals too warmly welcomed the *Ajijan nehar*, with the *Sadharani* of Chinsurah extending a neighbourly greeting. The *Sadharani* expressed pleasure that the Muslims of Bengal – who numbered nearly as much of the Hindus – had finally found someone to speak on their behalf. However, by the end of the year, the *Sadharani* changed its tone somewhat and issued a 'friendly' and somewhat incomprehensible rebuke to the *Ajijan*. The *Ajijan* did fairly well for the first couple of years before running out of steam in the third. Debts at the printer's had piled up, and even a shift to the famed Budhoday Press at Hooghly did not mend matters.[149]

After this apprenticeship, Mosharraf founded another periodical, the *Hitakari* in 1890, this time from the Mathurnath Press from Kumarkhali. Modelled on the lines of *Grambarta*, the *Hitakari* was vocal in drawing attention to the woes of the peasantry, and had a chequered career, printing first from Kumarkhali and then from Tangail. Despite the somewhat tangled history of its ownership and continuity, it was a true follower of the *Grambarta* and agitated relentlessly on behalf of the oppressed and the destitute. Recently, scholarly attention has been drawn to the linguistic register of the *Hitakari* and Mosharraf's championing of the Bengali language in the cause of nationalism.[150]

~

A Bend in History: Murshidabad

Situated 200 kilometres to the north of Calcutta and on the eastern bank of the river Hooghly, Murshidabad was the centre of Bengal's political and economic power before the rise of Calcutta. In the sixteenth and seventeenth centuries, it was the capital of the Bengal *subah* of the Mughal empire, and subsequently the seat of the Nawab of Bengal. Its primacy began to wane after the victory of the East India Company at the Battle of Plassey in 1757, following which its courts, treasury and revenue offices were shifted to Calcutta.

The history of printing in Murshidabad follows the familiar trajectory of an early start turning out to be a false dawn. In May 1840, Calcutta

[149] Chaudhuri, 'Mir Mosharraf Hossain'. [150] Khan, *Mir Mosharraf Hossain*.

newspapers reported with approval about the appearance of a new periodical in distant Murshidabad, the first of its kind in the provinces. Titled the *Murshidabad samvadpatri*, the weekly was edited by Gurudayal Choudhury and supported by Kumar Kishan Nath Roy. Long provides a little more context: ' . . . under the patronage of the late Rajah of Berhampore, who wished to improve his tenants by it'.[151] According to the *Calcutta Review*, there was also an English newspaper predating the Bengali: '(I)n 1838, an English Newspaper was begun there called the *Murshidabad News*, it met with a good circulation, the Court of Directors subscribed for 10 copies of it, but afterwards it became scurrilous and engaged in personal abuse, the consequence of which was that it became extinct in 1839.'[152] The *Murshidabad samvadpatri*, too, did not last long, having incurred the ire of the magistrate of Murshidabad.[153]

Despite quite an early start, print did not return till Murshidabad till the 1860s, when the Dhanasindhu Press of Nabinchandra Choudhury began operations in nearby Azimganj. The press printed both books and periodicals, and its *Biswamanoranjan*, a weekly which began in January 1862, may be considered to be the first periodical from Murshidabad in over two decades. The following January, the press issued another weekly, the *Samvad bharatbandhu*, edited by Nabakishore Sen. But the editor fell ill and died soon after, and the two periodicals merged in the portmanteau name *Bharatranjan* from July 1864. The press, too, shifted to Berhampore which would soon become a major centre of literary activity owing to the arrival of the novelist Bankimchandra Chattopadhyay as deputy magistrate.

In contrast to the other princely city of Burdwan, printing exploded in Murshidabad in the last third of the nineteenth century with a number of presses turning out a wide range of books and periodicals. Giving the Dhanasindhu Press stiff competition from the late 1860s was the Satyaratna Press (printer Ramnath Talukdar, prop. Sricharan Gooptu), also of Berhampore. However, it is noteworthy that few of the Murshidabad intelligentsia – such as Ramdas Sen or Loharam Siroratna – deigned to publish with local presses, preferring high-end Calcutta presses

---

[151] Long, *Descriptive Catalogue*, 67.   [152] 'The Banks of the Bhagirathi', 444.

[153] Brajendranath, *BSP 1818–68*, 74.

such as I. C. Bose's Stanhope Press or the New Sunskrit Press. An exception was the Sanskritist Ramnarayan Bidyaratna who had started his literary career by translating from the English and the French for Calcutta's Vernacular Literature Society in the 1850s. In two decades, he had become a staple of Murshidabad printers such as the Satyaratna Press, and then the Radharaman Press from 1873 which seemed to be a printer of exclusively Hindu and Vaisnava religious texts. The Radharaman Press was likely set up by Radharaman Ghosh of Dacca, a noted scholar of Vaisnava literature and sometime minister to the royal house of Tripura, in partnership with Ramnarayan himself. Ramnarayan seemed to have run the press more or less single-handedly, with his name appearing as both printer and publisher of the titles, most of which he authored himself.

Along with books, the periodical press continued to flourish in Murshidabad. The Dhanasindhu Press issued a news fortnightly in December 1866 titled *Murshidabad samvadsar*, and the weekly *Samavedak* in September 1873. The Satyaratna Press issued the monthly *Samalochoni* in April 1868 and the fortnightly *Madhukari* in 1870. But the longest-running troika of periodicals were the *Murshidabad patrika* (est. April 1872), the *Murshidabad pratinidhi* (est. March 1876) and the *Pratikar*. The last-named was launched at the same time as the *Pratinidhi*, as a direct rival. The print runs of both *Patrika* and the *Pratikar* were in the region of 500, and they were still going strong at the end of the century.

In April 1875, the Bishwabinod Press of Azimganj created history by issuing *Anathini*, the first-ever Bengali periodical to be edited by a woman, Thaokmani Devi. According to Brajendranath Bandyopadhyay, Thakomani was the 'young daughter' of the publisher of the periodical, Anukulchandra Chattopadhyay.[154] The first three issues of *Ananathini* were just eight pages long, sold at one anna and six paise, and had a print run of fifty. However, the fourth issue jumped to twenty-four pages, and was printed in an edition of 500, priced at four annas. Two more issues of the magazine appear to have been published.

What were the issues that exercised the periodical press in Murshidabad? From the evidence of the 'Native Newspaper Reports', we might see that in

[154] Brajendranath, *BSP 1868–1900*, 19.

1877, the *Murshidabad patrika* was commenting on questions such as land reforms and summary trials by magistrates, while the *Murshidabad pratinidhi* variously commented on the powers of magistrates, the need for vocational schools, famines and exports, and bribery in law courts. Interestingly, the issue of 1 March 1877 discussed 'the important service rendered to government by Native Newspapers. They give expression to thoughts and feelings, the wants and grievances of the natives, and thus enable the Rulers efficiently to carry out the duties of government.' The *Murshidabad patrika* of the same week adopted a similar tone, observing that 'however greatly the English might distrust us, we are exceedingly loyal to the British government'.[155] The following week, the *Pratinidhi* was commenting on issues ranging from the very local (politics among a college faculty), to the national (the civil procedure code bill) to the global (the advancing of Russia towards Kabul).

Among all the nodes of print surveyed so far, Murshidabad would seem to have the most diverse ecosystem of printing and publishing, though it is also among the least researched. The paucity of information on press ownership, for example, makes it difficult to identify the models of printing being employed. However, some tentative observations may be made from the information available. The vigour of the periodical press in Murshidabad seems to be at odds with the book trade, which was more limited and conservative in scope. In the last two decades of the nineteenth century especially, there was a distinct Vaisnavite and Puranic flavour to the imprints emanating from Murshidabad, much of which was owing to the figure of Ramnarayan Bidyaratna. The presswork wasn't anything to write home about, which might explain why the leading lights of the Murshidabad intelligentsia chose to publish from Calcutta presses.

In the case of one periodical, however, we are able to identify a stated agenda. This was the *Satsanga*, launched in Berhampore in April 1894 under the editorship of Satkari Bandyopadhyay. Swapan Basu has reported on the stop-start fate of the newspaper as well as its nomadic existence till it found a secure footing in Kirnahar in Birbhum district, where it was financially supported by a local zamindar. Despite the irregular existence, the *Satsanga*

[155] RNP, No. 10 of 1877, 5.

managed to retain its original complement of contributors, united in their aim of 'upholding the common weal . . . moulding the hearts and minds of wayward youth . . . dispelling superstition from society . . . and especially treating of the good counsel as well as the mysteries of the Hindu faith'.[156]

~

New Directions: Rungpore

After the *Murshidabad sambadpatri* of 1840, it took another seven years for the next Bengali newspaper to emerge from the districts. This was the *Rangpur bartabaha*, a weekly that was launched in August 1847 in the eastern Bengal town and district of Rungpore. Not a great deal is known about the contents of the paper, but the role of the local zamindar Kalichandra Roychowdhury in supporting the *Bartabaha* was one of the earliest instances of a landowner promoting the nascent periodical press. Kalichandra also famously announced a cash award for an original play assailing polygamy among the Kulin Brahmin. The playwright Ramnarayan Tarkaratna won the award of fifty rupees for the manuscript of *Kulin kulsarbasba* in 1855, and prompted the Rev. James Long to devote an approving paragraph to the work in his 1855 *Catalogue*: 'Designed like Uncle Tom's Cabin, by pointing out the evils of system lead to a remedy being applied.'[157] Long also noted the appearance of the *Bartabaha*, writing: 'Commenced under the patronage of an enlightened Zamindar there Kali Chandra Ray, the first native paper that took an interest in native population: Female education is advocated in it.'[158]

The first editor of the newspaper was Gurucharan Ray. After his death in 1851, Nilambar Mukhopadhyay took over the editorship. It had a print run of 100 and an annual subscription rate of six rupees (four rupees if paid in advance).[159] After coming out for ten years, the *Bartabaha* became one of the first newspapers in India to be shut down on account of Viceroy Canning's 'gagging act' of 1857. After the death of Kalichandra, the newspaper resumed under the name *Rangpur dikprakash* from April 1860, this

---

[156] Basu, *Sangbad-samayikpatre*, 16. [157] Long, *Descriptive Catalogue*, 13.
[158] Ibid., 69. [159] Mamoon, *Purbo banglaar songbad-samayikpatra*, 43.

time under the auspices of Sambhuchandra Roychowdhury, a zamindar from Kakiniya in Rungpore, and Madhusudan Bhattacharya as editor. Sambhuchandra went one better than Kalichandra by setting up a press in its name, the Sambhuchandra Jantra, which printed both books and periodicals. Under new management, the *Rangpur dikprakash* became one of the longest-running newspapers in Bengal. Madhusudan Bhattacharya was succeeded as editor by Harashankar Maitreya.

According to Swapan Basu, the paper was progressive in its outlook, opposing child marriage and polygamy. Despite being dependent on the patronage of the landowners, it did not become their mouthpiece.[160] Print runs were modest, varying between 250 (1877) and 180 (1899). Muntasir Mamoon has estimated that the *Dikprakash* ran at least till 1884,[161] but the annual returns of presses and newspapers in the Bengal Presidency show that the newspaper was published well into the 1890s, when it was kept in circulation by Mahimaranjan, the adoptive son of Kalichandra. The newspaper appears to have folded sometime in early 1899, after coming out uninterruptedly for nearly four decades.

In his magisterial biography of the reformer Ramtanu Lahiri, Sibnath Sastri notes that Rungpore had emerged as an important centre of national regeneration following Raja Rammohan Roy's residency there from 1809–14. A visit by the viceroy William Bentinck in 1832 helped catalyse the rise of English education in Rungpore. Sastri considers the beginning of printing in Rungpore as part of the general project of modernisation in the region, which was given a further impetus by the founding of the Rungpore Brahmo Samaj in 1868.[162]

~

---

[160] Basu, *Sangbad-samayikpatre*, 11.

[161] Mamoon, *Purbo banglaar songbad-samayikpatra*, 44.

[162] Sastri, *Ramtanu lahiri*, 174–5.

Conclusion: The End of a Beginning?

In this brief study, I have tried to narrate a history of print that focusses attention on some of its less studied and understood pathways in colonial Bengal. Thanks to the existing scholarship, we have some understanding of how print evolved and accelerated in locations like Serampore and Calcutta, and how it was linked to a project of technologising and disciplining knowledge. The missionaries, in particular, inaugurated a set of textual practices that constituted a sharp break from the oral and scribal protocols that obtained over much of India. This may, in part, explain the lack of success of the missionary *textual* project, as opposed to the undoubted success of the infrastructure of print built by missionary initiative. As we have seen in Chapter 1, the missionaries laboured mightily to create an elaborate network of print that failed to fulfil its primary objective. But it was the secondary, and often unintended, consequences of the project that would have enormous impact on textual practices over the whole of South Asia.

The case was somewhat different in Calcutta, where print, though closely linked with the colonial project, also participated in other forms of textual production. While institutions such as the Fort William College, and to a lesser extent, the CSBS, enacted a textual regime of power and disciplining, there was also a more promiscuous arena for print to participate in. In this arena, print was able to negotiate a dialogic relationship with script, and even orality, and it was in this arena that the indigenisation and domestication of print could take place. At the same time, such negotiations could only take place within the framework of the city's economic practice, within the flows of its capital and human resources. The print-shops that were situated within it as well as its products were subject to the rules of the marketplace in general and the nascent book trade in particular.

In contrast, the mofussil press was cut from a different cloth. The early presses arose out of traditional models of patronage and philanthropy, and found it difficult to switch to a primarily transactional mode of circulation. While the city presses had access to buyers or subscribers both in the city and the hinterland, district presses were circumscribed by their limited reach and distance from the city. True, there were exceptions like the *Somprakash*, but Dwarkanath's newspaper had begun life in Calcutta and had been able to build a substantial subscribers' base before moving out of the city. In such circumstances, only those with ready access to liquidity or willingness to bear losses could last the course. Given such constraints, the district press depended heavily on patronage or voluntary labour. While the presses which printed books could afford to operate on a commercial basis (e.g. Chandroday Press, Tamohar Press, Budhoday Press, Satyaratna Press), the periodical press was overwhelmingly a labour of love. Not surprisingly, it was often sustained by the efforts of an educated middle-class intelligentsia, comprising school and college teachers, scholars, writers and government officials – in other words, those who already had a living wage. In their efforts, we might see a conscious attempt to reimagine a public sphere in the hinterland independent of that of the big city.

On occasions, as with the *Grambarta prakashika*, the mofussil press took the city press to task for aligning with the interests of the landed gentry. As Swapan Basu argues, the conflict between the zamindars and the *ryots* or the peasantry polarised the periodical press, particularly during the agrarian uprisings in Pabna district in eastern Bengal, in 1873. Journalists who had formerly defended the ryots during the indigo uprising a decade ago – such as Sishir Kumar Ghosh, the founder of the famous *Amrita bazar patrika* – now turned apologists for the landowners, prompting the *Grambarta* to thunder: 'Our beloved Amrita Bazar has deserted the countryside for the capital city, how will they any longer feel the woes of the stricken peasantry?'[163]

What were the economics of running a press in the mofussil? Despite the near-complete lack of data in this regard, Muntasir Mamoon has been able to salvage some figures. Mamoon informs us that an advertisement of the Bangala Press in the *Dhaka prakash* of 1863 quotes a price of five rupees for composing and printing a forme in Bengali, and six rupees in English. In 1870, the Sulabh Press advertised rates between four and ten rupees. To put this in perspective, the monthly salary of a press compositor in Dacca could vary between fifteen and thirty rupees. Postage charges were high, and could often be higher than printing costs.[164] Against this, the yearly subscription revenue of a newspaper

[163] Basu, *Sangbad-samayikpatre*, 50.

[164] Mamoon, 'Unish shatake samvad-samayikpatrer kathamo, sthaitva, prachar, o bibaran', in Mamoon ed., *Dui shatake*, 15–17.

such as the *Rangpur dikprakash* (advance subscription: four rupees; average circulation: 200) could be in the region of 800–1,000 rupees. Additional revenue could accrue from advertisements. Though these figures are not enough for us to arrive at any firm conclusion, it would not be too far off the mark to say that most such presses would have struggled to make ends meet.

In one of the earliest studies on the periodical press (1917) Kedarnath Majumdar reports how the beginning of the periodical press in the mofussil led to a petition to Lord Dalhousie asking for a 'uniform rate of postage' across India. This led to postal reforms in 1853, and a lowering of rates to half an anna for letters and papers. Majumdar argues that the rationalisation of postal rates gave a fillip to the newspaper press in the mofussil, but this was short-lived owing to Canning's Gagging Act following the 1857 uprising.[165] But it was with the launching of the *Somprakash* from Calcutta in November 1858 and the *Dhaka prakash* from Dacca in March 1861 that the mofussil really began to come into its own. For 1873, Majumder calculated a total of eighty-one current periodicals, out of which as many as forty-two were being printed from the mofussil, and thirty-nine from Calcutta.[166] For the same year, Ramgati Nyayratna calculated that if there were sixty current periodicals and newspapers (not counting almanacs) in Bengal, their cumulative circulation would be 20,000 copies, at an average of 300 copies per periodical.[167]

We have some ideas about circulation figures from 1877, when the weekly 'Reports on Native Newspapers' began to print runs of some of the more active newspapers (see Table 6). For obvious reasons, the Calcutta-based papers logged the highest print runs, with the weekly *Bangabasi* heading the list at 25,000 (January 1899) followed by the weekly *Basumati* at 15,000 (January 1899). The *Hindi bangabasi* too registered a print run of 6,500 during the same period. Among the monthlies, the pioneering *Bharat shramajibi* (est. 1874) reached a circulation of 15,000 at the height of its popularity. But among the weeklies from outside Calcutta, only the *Somprakash* was just about able to reach the thousand-mark. In the Burdwan Division, only the *Education Gazette* consistently achieved a print run of around 800 in the 1880s

---

[165] Majumdar, *Bangla samayik sahitya*, 189–91.   [166] Ibid., 192.
[167] Nyayratna, *Bangala bhasha*, 155.

before rising to around 1,350 towards the end of the century. The *Bardhaman sanjivani*, despite its long and distinguished career, did not surpass 300. Murshidabad fared slightly better, with the figures of the leading newspapers consistently hovering around the 500–600 mark. The rest of the newspapers and periodicals – mostly weeklies – were rarely able to surpass the 500 mark, with the figures seeming to decline as we move towards the east. In January 1899, in the Rajshahi Division, for instance, the *Hindu ranjika* had a run of 243, and the veteran of four decades, the *Rangpur dikprakash*, a run of only 180. The situation was marginally better in the Dacca Division, where weeklies such as the *Dhaka prakash* had a print run of 2,400 and the *Charu mihir* of Mymensingh, 900.

However, what we do not have an idea about is the print run of periodicals and magazines that are not newspapers. While the newspaper in the mofussil may have declined in numbers and print run over the last third of the nineteenth century, the overall tally for both newspapers and magazines continued to rise across the decades. The following is the tally of new newspapers/magazines coming out from the districts in the Bengali language:

> 1841–49: 6   1850–59: 11   1861–69: 38
> 1871–79: 95   1880–89: 89   1890–1900: 69

Again, these are very broad figures, but what they do indicate is a peaking of mofussil printing in the 1880s, and then a gradual tapering off in the last two decades of the century. Similar indicators are available from Muntasir Mamoon's study on newspapers in eastern Bengal where there is a marked falling-off in the last decade of the nineteenth century. Of the 78 newspapers surveyed between 1847 and 1905, only 12 were founded in the fifteen-year period from 1891 to 1905. Magazines fare somewhat better, the corresponding figure being 47 out of a total of 158, though the total for the previous decade, 1881–90, is 26 for newspapers and 55 for magazines.[168] Thus, it is clear that the falling-off begins in the last decade of the century, decisively for newspapers and perceptibly for magazines.

[168] Mamoon, *Purbo banglaar songbad-samayikpatra*, 39–41.

Several reasons may be suggested for this. Firstly, most of the periodicals surveyed above depended on direct and indirect patronage and philanthropy. The initial excitement and sense of novelty that may have spurred such philanthropy could not be sustained in the long run. Secondly, the Vernacular Press Act of 1878 (repealed in 1881), which imposed restrictions upon the contents of vernacular periodicals, led to the closure of many publications. Most, such as the *Education Gazette*, maintained a discreet silence while the likes of *Somprakash* received a rap on the knuckles. It is not a coincidence that the press act was passed just a year after the reports on native newspapers began to circulate confidentially among the government, and could well have conveyed an impression that the 'native press' was under some degree of surveillance. A third reason, suggested by Mamoon, was the impact of the Brahmo movement in eastern Bengal, which resulted in the founding of a number of societies and their organs.[169] This reached its peak between the 1860s and the 1880s but tapered off in the last decade of the century.

How do we explain the low print runs in the mofussil, at a time when newspapers in Calcutta were able to sustain five-figure print runs? In Calcutta, periodicals were sustained by a relatively wealthy middle class that was also becoming aware of its own place in the world, especially as inhabitants of one of the major cities of the British Empire. The large print runs would translate into substantial subscription revenues, which would ensure a steady supply of capital. Another considerable source of revenue would be advertisements. In the mofussil, on the other hand, the cycle of low print runs and low subscription collections made access to capital almost impossible, and the periodical could necessarily have to subsist on and by the margins. A recurring complaint by editors of mofussil papers would be the difficulties faced in realising subscription dues – not everyone could afford to be a Dwarkanath Bidyabhushan, whose stated policy was not to despatch a single copy of *Somprakash* if the subscription was not paid in advance. The lack of ready venture capital would also be an impediment in modernising the print-house, as well as the bindery. City presses were able to invest in the latest technology and equipment, whereas most

[169] Ibid., 4

mofussil presses were acquired second-hand. The mofussil was also dependent on the city for paper, type and press furniture, a state of affairs that by and large obtains to the present day.

This study stops at the point when a regional telling of the story of print is, perhaps, no longer possible. As print began to grapple with the project of imagining the Indian 'nation', the periodical press increasingly shifted its focus from socio-cultural to political issues. The local and the regional still remained important, but the discourse of nationalism and anti-colonialism demanded a heightened order of engagement. New networks of affiliation and conflict were taking shape, both within the boundaries of India, and outside. A different telling awaits the history of print during this period.

~

Epilogue: The Many Beatitudes of Kangal Harinath

On a hot summer's day sometime in 1880, a group of young men and boys might have been seen fanning themselves vigorously under a tree in the village Kumarkhali. They had been writing copy and typesetting for the *Grambarta prakashika* newspaper, but the heat and humidity had driven them out of the printing-house. The group comprised two newly anointed editors, Jaladhar Sen and Akshaykumar Maitreya, both local boys who had just started their professional careers away from the village. But it was summer vacation and they were back home doing what they loved best, messing around in the print-house and preparing the newspaper for the press. The rest of the company consisted of the headmaster of the village school, the printer of *Grambarta*, and a number of 'printer's devils' who worked in the press.[170]

As they lay in the shadow of the tree, the group began to get restless. What shall we do, said the printer's devils. Shall we form a *baul* group, asked the young Akshay, who had been preparing for his law degree. That morning, Lalon Shah, the most legendary of all *bauls*,[171] had visited Kangal Harinath in his hovel. He had sung a few songs that had moved the group but also left them mystified. How difficult would it be to write a *baul* song? Young Akshay obviously thought nothing of it, and started extemporising lyrics as Jaladhar scribbled the lines on paper meant for presswork. Soon, a very passable song about the path of truth in the byways of life had taken shape. But it was not enough to just to write the lyrics, a lyricist would also have to found who would lend his name to the lines. Another quicksilver inspiration from young Akshay and the name Fikirchand was hit upon.

The next thing was to take the song to the Kangal. He was writing in his hovel and looked up as the 'regiment' trooped in. As the group raised its collective voice in song, the Kangal became transformed; he rose from his

---

[170] The epilogue is based upon Jaladhar Sen's account of Harinath's life: see Sen, *Kangal harinath*, 22–61.

[171] Bauls are seekers of truth who belong to a syncretic tradition drawn from Sufi and Sahajiya practice in greater Bengal. They do not follow any established religion and the *baul* song is the most visible marker of their repertoire.

seat and began to dance. When the song ended, the Kangal said, 'This song will conquer the land. But we need to write more songs. Let me write one as well. Akshay, pen, paper!' The Kangal hummed a bit, and then began to sing. This time it was a song about a harassed cowherd who kept losing his cattle.

That evening, a strange procession could be seen in Kumarkhali village. The printer's devils, wearing long robes and pantomime beards and playing assorted instruments, did a round of the village, singing their new songs. The whole village followed at their heels. Within a few days, the people of nearly a score of villages in and around Kumarkhali were humming the songs. More songs were needed for the new group. Young Akshay said, I can't do this anymore. Can you not see that a new force has been unleashed? Only the Kangal can stand at the head of this tide. Unexpectedly, Prafulla, the printer of the press came forward. Who would have known he was capable of such emotion? A new song was ready in a quarter of an hour. When the troupe sallied forth with their new offering, villagers from all over were waiting in the sun to listen to them.

As the group sang and danced their way through the countryside, the Kangal Harinath saw in them the possibility of a social regeneration. 'The sweetness of Akshay and Prafulla's songs convinced me that we could do some good, by singing these songs of truth, knowledge, and love and its mysteries,' he wrote. He set himself at the head of the group, and a strange, new music flowed out of Kumarkhali, enchanting both high and low. It flowed across the rivers and villages of lower Bengal, drawing crowds of tens of thousands of Hindus and Muslims wherever it went. Invitations came from near and far, from Rajshahi, Natore, Rungpore, Dacca, Mymensingh, Faridpur and Goalanda. The group was on the road for days on end, as their music drew ecstatic crowds who would not let them leave. They seemed to be everywhere, even at the tumultuous farewell given to Viceroy Ripon as he made his last railway journey from Darjeeling to Calcutta.

How do we accommodate a story such as this within the limits of our disciplinary practice? The ease with which the village pressmen were able to dissolve and overflow the boundaries between script, print and orality is a salutary lesson to those of us who traffic in niches and pigeonholes. At every bend, the story forces us to reconsider our carefully constructed fields of textual practice, and the technological determinisms that underpin our scholarly protocols. It alerts us to the possibility of a life of print outside itself – the epiphanies of print.

Abbreviations

The following abbreviations have been used in the text and notes:

BSP	*Bangla samayikpatra*
CCTBS	Calcutta Christian Tract and Book Society
CSBS	Calcutta School-Book Society
SSC vols. 1–3	*Sahitya-sadhak charitmala*
SSK vols. 1–5	*Sangbadpatre sekaler katha*

References

Archival Sources and Reports

Annual Reports of the Calcutta School-Book Society, 1819–57

Baptist Missionary Society archives, Angus Library and Archive, Regent's Park College, Oxford

Bengal Library Catalogue of Books, 1868–1947

Reports on the Administration of Bengal, 1866–85

Reports on Native Newspapers, 1874–99

Newspapers and Periodicals

Halisahar patrika, 1871–82

Sadharani, 1874–76

Somprakash, 1862–63

Published Sources (English)

'Appendix A', *General Report on Public Instruction in the Lower Provinces of the Bengal Presidency for 1856–57* (Calcutta: Calcutta Gazette Office, 1857), 58–64.

'Appendix I, Education of Natives', *Appendix to the Report from the Select Committee of the House of Commons on the Affairs of the East India Company* (London: 1833), 395–548.

'Authentic Account of the Saadhs', *The Missionary Register for 1819* (London: L. B. Seeley, 1819), 86–91.

'The Banks of the Bhagirathi', *Calcutta Review*, vol. 6 (July–Dec. 1846), 398–448.

Basak, N. L. 'Origin and Role of the Calcutta School Book Society in Promoting the Cause of Education in India, Especially Vernacular Education in Bengal', *Bengal Past and Present*, vol. 77, no. 145 (Jan.–Jun. 1959), 30–69.

Bhabha, Homi. 'Signs Taken for Wonders: Questions of Ambivalence and Authority under a Tree outside Delhi, May 1817', *Critical Enquiry*, vol. 12, no.1 (1985), 144–65.

Bhadra, Gautam. 'Pictures in Celestial and Worldly Time: Illustrations in Nineteenth-Century Bengali Almanacs', in Partha Chatterjee, Tapati Guha-Thakurta and Bodhisattva Kar, eds. *New Cultural Histories of India: Materiality and Practices* (New Delhi: Oxford University Press, 2014), 275–316.

Blumhardt, J. F. *Catalogue of Bengali Printed Books in the Library of the British Museum* (London: Trustees of the British Museum, 1886).

Burnell, A. C. and Henry Yule. *A Glossary of Colloquial Anglo-Indian Words and Phrases. Hobson-Jobson* (London: John Murray, 1886).

'The Calcutta Native Press', *Calcutta Christian Observer*, no. 2, n.s. (February 1840), 57–66.

'Calcutta School Book Society', *Calcutta Monthly Journal. Asiatic News. 1836* (Calcutta: Samuel Smith, 1837), 171–2.

Carey, Eustace. *Memoir of William Carey, D.D.* (Hartford: Canfield and Robins, 1837).

Carey, William. *A Grammar of the Mahratta Language, to Which Are Added Dialogues on Familiar Subjects* (Serampore: Mission Press, 1805).

Chakravorty, Swapan. 'Purity and Print: A Note on Nineteenth Century Bengali Prose', in Abhijit Gupta and Swapan Chakravorty, eds. *Print Areas Book History in India* (Delhi: Permanent Black, 2004), 197–226.

Das Gupta, Uma. 'The Indian Press 1870–1880: A Small World of Journalism', *Modern Asian Studies*, vol. 11, no. 2 (1977), 213–35.

De, Amalendu. 'Publication of Text-Books in Bengali: A Movement for Child Education in Nineteenth Century Bengal', in Rakhal Bhattacharya, ed. *David Hare Bicentenary Volume 1975–76* (Calcutta: David Hare Bicentenary of Birth Celebration Committee, 1976), 72–93.

Finkelstein, David. *Movable Types: Roving Creative Printers of the Victorian World* (Oxford: Oxford University Press, 2018).

Ghosh, Anindita. 'An Uncertain "Coming of the Book": Print Cultures in Colonial India', *Book History*, vol. 6 (2003), 23–55.

Gupta, Abhijit. 'The Calcutta School-Book Society and the Production of Knowledge', in *English Studies in Africa*, vol. 57, no., no. 1 (May 2014), 55–65.

Gupta, Abhijit. 'What Really Happened under a Tree outside Delhi, May 1817', in Swapan Chakravorty and Abhijit Gupta, eds. *Founts of Knowledge: Book History in India* (New Delhi: Orient Blackswan, 2016), 334–52.

Kocchar, Rajesh. *English Education in India 1715–1835: Half-Caste, Missionary and Secular Stages* (Abingdon and New York: Routledge, 2021).

'Literature and the Press', *Annual Report of the Administration of the Bengal Presidency, for 1878–79* (Calcutta: Bengal Secretariat Press, 1869).

'Literary and Philosophical Intelligence', *The Supplementary Number to the Twenty-First Volume of the Monthly Magazine*, vol. 21, no. 3 (1 April 1806).

Long, James. *A Descriptive Catalogue of Bengali Works* (Calcutta: Sanders & Cones, 1855).

Long, James. 'On Vernacular Christian Literature', in *Proceedings of a General Conference on Bengal Protestant Missionaries* (Calcutta: Baptist Mission Press, 1855), 124–34.

Long, James. *Selection from the Records of the Bengal Government, No. 33* (Calcutta: John Gray, 1859).

Memoir Relative to the Translation of the Scriptures into Certain of the Oriental Languages (Serampore: Mission Press, 1808).

'Memoir Relative to Translations, Addressed to the Society', *The Panoplist*, vol. 5, no. 11 (April 1813), 523–7.

Memoir Relative to the Translations of the Sacred Scriptures (Dunstable: J. W. Morris, 1808).

'Minute by the Hon'ble T. B. Macaulay, Dated the 2nd February 1835'. www.columbia.edu/itc/mealac/pritchett/00generallinks/macaulay/ txt_minute_education_1835.html. Accessed 22 May 2021.

Mitra, Samarpita. *Periodicals, Readers and the Making of a Modern Literary Culture* (Leiden: Brill, 2020).

Mohanty, Sachidananda. *Periodical Press and Colonial Modernity. Odisha 1866–1936* (New Delhi: Oxford University Press, 2016).

Monthly Circular Letters Relative to the Missions of India, vol. 6 (Serampore: Mission Press, 1813).

'Native Ingenuity', *Asiatic Journal and Monthly Miscellany*, vol. 37 (1842), 26–7.

Natrajan, S. *A History of the Press in India* (Bombay: Asia Publishing House, 1962).

Oddie, Geoffrey. *Missionaries, Rebellion and Proto-Nationalism: James Long of Bengal 1804–87* (London and New York: Routledge, 1991).

'On the Effect of the Native Press in India', *The Friend of India*, Quarterly Series, no. 1 (September 1820), 119–40.

Orsini, Francesca. *Print and Pleasure: Popular Literature and Entertaining Fictions in Colonial North India* (Ranikhet: Permanent Black, 2009).

Pal, Bipin Chandra. *Memories of my Life and Times* (Calcutta: Modern Book Agency, 1932).

Peterson, J. C. K. *Bengal District Gazetteers: Burdwan* (Calutta: Bengal Secretariat Book Depot, 1910).

Ray, Deeptanil and Abhijit Gupta. 'The Newspaper and the Periodical Press in Colonial India', in Joanne Shattock, ed. *Journalism and the*

Periodical Press in Nineteenth-Century Britain (Cambridge University Press, 2017), 245–62.

'Report of the Director of Public Instruction', *General Report on Public Instruction in the Lower Provinces of the Bengal Presidency for 1856–57* (Calcutta: Calcutta Gazette Office, 1857).

Roy, Tapti. *Print and Publishing in Colonial Bengal: The Journey of Bidyasundar* (London and New York: Routledge, 2019).

Scott-Waring, John. *A Letter to the Rev. John Owen* (London: 1808).

Sengupta, Parna. *Pedagogy for Religion: Missionary Education and the Fashioning of Hindus and Muslims in Bengal* (Berkeley, New York and London: University of California Press, 2011).

Sen Gupta, Sankar. *Folklorists of Bengal* (Calcutta: Indian Publications, 1965).

Shaw, Graham. 'The Cuttack Mission Press and Early Oriya Printing', *British Library Journal* (1977), 29–43.

Shaw, Graham. *Printing in Calcutta till 1800: A Description and Checklist of Printing in late 18th Century Calcutta* (London: The Bibliographical Society, 1981).

Shaw, Graham. 'South Asia', in Jonathan Rose and Simon Eliot, eds. *A Companion to the History of the Book* (London: Wiley-Blackwell, 2007), 126–37.

Smith, George. *The Life of William Carey, D.D.* (London: John Murray, 1885).

Stark, Ulrike. *An Empire of Books: The Nawal Kishore Press and the Diffusion of the Printer Word in Colonial India* (Ranikhet: Permanent Black, 2009).

Stennett, Samuel. *Memoirs of the Life of the Rev. William Ward* (London: 1825).

Tenth Memoir Respecting the Translations of the Sacred Scriptures by the Serampore Brethren (London, et al.: 1834).

Venkatachalapathy, A. R. *The Province of the Book: Scholars, Scribes, and Scribblers in Colonial Tamilnadu* (Ranikhet: Permanent Black, 2012).

Yates, William. *Memoirs of Mr John Chamberlain, Late Missionary in India* (Calcutta and London: Baptist Mission Press, Wightman and Cramp, 1826).

Published Sources (Bengali)

Bagal, Jogeshchandra. 'Bankimchandra chattopadhyay', *Bankim rachana-bali*, vol. 1 (Kolkata: Sahitya Samsad, 1953).

Bandyopadhyay, Brajendranath, *Bangla samayikpatra 1818–1868* (Kolkata: Bamgiya Sahitya Parishat, 1936; 1972).

Bandyopadhyay, Brajendranath, *Bangla samayikpatra 1868–1900* (Kolkata: Bamgiya Sahitya Parishat, 1951; 1977).

Bandyopadhyay, Brajendranath. *Sahitya-sadhak-charitmala*, vols. 1–3 (Kolkata: Bamgiya Sahitya Parishat, 2017).

Bandyopadhhay, Brajendranath. *Sangbadpatre sekaler katha*, vols. 1–3 (Kolkata: Bamgiya Sahitya Parishat, 1932, 1933, 1935).

Basu, Swapan. ed. *Sangbad-samayikpatre unish shataker bangalisamaj*, vol. 1 (Kolkata: Deep Prakashan, 2000).

Bhadra, Gautam. *Nyara battlaay jay kobar?* (Kolkata: Chaatim, 2011).

Bhudeb Charit, vol. 1 (Kolkata: India Press, 1917).

Chaudhuri, Abul Ahsan. 'Sampadak Mir Mosharraf Hossain', in *Kali o kalam* (21 September 2015). https://tinyurl.com/22v5mv3v. Accessed 5 June 2021.

Datta, Sandip. *Bangla samayikpatrer itibritta 1818–1899* (Kolkata: Gangchil, 2012).

Ghosh, Binay. *Samayikpatre banglar samajchitra*, vols. 1, 3, 4 and 6. Vol. 1 (Kolkata: Bengal Publishers, 1960); vol. 3 (Kolkata: Bikshan, 1960); vol. 4 (Kolkata: Patha Bhaban, 1960); Vol. 6 (Kolkata: Papyrus, 1983).

Khan, Samsuzzaman. *Mir Mosharraf Hossain: natun tathye natun bhasye* (Dhaka: Abashar Prakashan, 2003).

Khastagir, Asish. *Unish shataker bangla chapakhana* (Kolkata: Sopan, 2014).

Kumar, Jnanendranath. *Bangsha parichay*, vols. 1 and 2 (Kolkata: 1934, 1921).

Maitreya, Akshaykumar. 'Akshaykumar Maitreyar banghsa pairchay', in Nagendranath Basu, *Banger jatia itihas: barendra brahman-bibaran* (Kolkata: 1927).

Majumdar, Kedarnath. *Bangla samayik sahitya*, vol. 1 (Mymensingh: Research House, 1917).

Mamoon, Muntasir. *Dui shatake bangla samvad-samayikpatra* (Kolkata: Pustak Bipani, 2000).

Mamoon, Muntasir. *Unish shotoke purbo banglaar songbad-samayikpatra* (Kolkata: Dey's, 1997).

Mitra, Sudhirkumar. *Hooghly jelar itihas o bangasamaj*, vol. 2 (Kolkata: Mitrani, 1975).

Nyayratna, Ramgati. *Bangala bhasha o sahitya bisayak prabandha* (Hooghly: Budhoday Press, 1873).

Sarkar, Giridhari. 'Bardhaman raj o bardhamaner prakashana', *Anandabazar Patrika* (24 February 2019). www.anandabazar.com/editorial/article-on-publication-house-of-bardhaman-royal-family-1.957144. Accessed 31 Jan. 2021.

Sastri, Haraprasad. *Haraprasad sastri rachana-sangraha*, vol. 2, eds. Satyajt Chaudhuri et al. (Kolkata: Paschimbanga rajya pustak parshad, n.d.).

Sastri, Sibnath. *Atmacharit* (Kolkata: Brahmo Samaj, 1918).

Sastri, Sibnath. *Ramtanu lahiri o tatkalin bangasamaj* (Kolkata: New Age Publishers, 2007; 1904).

Sen, Jaladhar. *Kangal harinath jiban katha* (Kolkata: Bengali Medical Library, 1913).

Sen, Sukumar. 'Battalar boi', in Chittaranjan Bandyopdhyay, ed. *Dui shotoker bangla mudron o prokashon* (Kolkata: Ananda, 1981).

Acknowledgements

Caroline Davis, Debraj Ghatak, Devalina Mookerjee, Giridhari Sarkar, Graham Shaw, Richard Kossow, Sanjukta Roy, Suchismita Ghosh, Susnato Chowdhury, the two reviewers.

The staff at the Angus Library and Archive, Regent's Park College, Oxford; British Library, London; the Cambridge University Library, Cambridge; Carey Library and Research Institute, Serampore; CRASSH, Cambridge; National Library of India, Kolkata.

Project members of the 'Two Centuries of Print in India' project at the British Library, London. Colleagues and students at the Department of English, Jadavpur University, the Jadavpur University Press and the School of Cultural Texts and Records.

The managers and trustees of the American Bibliographical Society; the Bibliographical Society; Charles Wallace India Trust; University Grants Commission, India.

Cambridge Elements ≡

Publishing and Book Culture

SERIES EDITOR
Samantha Rayner
University College London

Samantha Rayner is a Reader in UCL's Department of
Information Studies. She is also Director of UCL's Centre for
Publishing, co-Director of the Bloomsbury CHAPTER
(Communication History, Authorship, Publishing, Textual
Editing and Reading) and co-editor of the Academic Book of
the Future BOOC (Book as Open Online Content) with UCL
Press.

ASSOCIATE EDITOR
Leah Tether
University of Bristol

Leah Tether is Professor of Medieval Literature and Publishing
at the University of Bristol. With an academic background in
medieval French and English literature and a professional
background in trade publishing, Leah has combined her
expertise and developed an international research profile in
book and publishing history from manuscript to digital.

About the Series

This series aims to fill the demand for easily accessible, quality texts available for teaching and research in the diverse and dynamic fields of Publishing and Book Culture. Rigorously researched and peer-reviewed Elements will be published under themes, or 'Gatherings'. These Elements should be the first check point for researchers or students working on that area of publishing and book trade history and practice: we hope that, situated so logically at Cambridge University Press, where academic publishing in the UK began, it will develop to create an unrivalled space where these histories and practices can be investigated and preserved.

Cambridge Elements ☰

Publishing and Book Culture
Colonial and Post-Colonial Publishing

Gathering Editor: Caroline Davis

Caroline Davis is Senior Lecturer in the Oxford International Centre for Publishing at Oxford Brookes University. She is the author of *Creating Postcolonial Literature: African Writers and British Publishers* (Palgrave, 2013), the editor of *Print Cultures: A Reader in Theory and Practice* (Macmillan, 2019) and co-editor of *The Book in Africa: Critical Debates* (Palgrave, 2015).

A full series listing is available at: www.cambridge.org/EPBC

Printed in the United States
by Baker & Taylor Publisher Services